GOTHENBURG TF
2023-2024

A Guide to the Natural and Cultural Attractions of Sweden's Second Largest City. Everything you Need to Know Before Planning a Trip to Gothenburg

GENEVA WALKER

All rights reserved. No part of this publication may be reproduced, distributed, or transmitted in any form or by any means, including
photocopying, recording, or other electronic or mechanical methods, without the prior written permission of the publisher, except in the case of brief quotations embodied in critical reviews and certain other noncommercial uses permitted by copyright law.

Copyright © Geneva Walker, 2023.

Table of Contents

INTRODUCTION **6**

    HOW I RANDOMLY CHOSE GOTHENBURG AS MY NEXT DESTINATION 6

    WHY VISIT GOTHENBURG? 11

    WHEN TO LEAVE AND WHAT TO PACK? 18

    HOW TO GET THERE AND AROUND 25

    PRACTICAL ADVICE AND IMPORTANT INFORMATION 32

        Getting there and around 32

        Where to stay 33

        What to see and do 34

CHAPTER 1: HISTORY AND CULTURE **36**

    THE BEGINNINGS AND EVOLUTION OF GOTHENBURG 36

    THE CULTURAL AND CREATIVE SCENE IN GOTHENBURG 44

    FESTIVALS AND EVENTS IN GOTHENBURG 50

    THE LOCAL CUISINE AND PECULIARITIES IN GOTHENBURG 54

        Seafood restaurants 54

        Michelin restaurants 55

        Affordable bistros 57

        Classic restaurants 58

CHAPTER 2 .... **60**

ATTRACTIONS AND SIGHTSEEING 60

    The Feskekörka fish market and the seafood restaurants ... 60

    The Feskekörka fish market 61

    Liseberg amusement park and the roller coasters 68

    The Skansen Kronan Fortress and the panoramic views 71

    The Haga district and the huge cinnamon buns 75

    The Gothenburg Museum of Art and the Nordic collections 79

CHAPTER 3: NATURE AND OUTDOORS 84

    THE SLOTTSSKOGEN PARK AND THE ZOO 85

    THE BOTANICAL GARDEN AND THE GREENHOUSES 91

    THE SOUTHERN ARCHIPELAGO AND THE CAR-FREE ISLANDS 95

    THE DELSJÖN LAKE AND THE HIKING PATHWAYS 99

    THE ÄLVSBORG FORTRESS AND THE BOAT TRIPS 104

CHAPTER 4: SHOPPING AND ENTERTAINMENT 112

    THE NORDSTAN RETAIL COMPLEX AND THE FASHION SHOPS 114

    THE AVENYN BOULEVARD AND THE NIGHTLIFE VENUES 117

    MAGASINSGATAN STREET AND THE DESIGN STORES 123

    THE SALUHALLEN MARKET HALL AND THE DELICATESSEN STALLS 126

    THE BACKA TEATER AND THE CURRENT PERFORMANCES 131

CHAPTER 5 134

3-7 Days Itinerary in Gothenburg 134

    Day 1: Discover the city center 134

    Day 2: Explore additional museums and parks 135

    Day 3: Visit Skansen Kronan and Haga 137

    Day 4: Visit the archipelago 138

    Day 5: Visit Gothenburg's environs 139

    Day 6: Visit the West Coast 140

    Day 7: Visit Trollhättan and Vänersborg 141

CHAPTER 6 146

Accommodation and Dining 146

The top hotels and hostels in Gothenburg for varied budgets and interests 148

    Budget accommodation in Gothenburg 149

    Mid-range accommodation in Gothenburg 151

    Luxury accommodation in Gothenburg 154

The Best Restaurants and Cafés in Gothenburg for various cuisines and events 158

    Swedish cuisine 158

    International cuisine 159

    Trendy places 160

    Cafes 161

CHAPTER 7: PRACTICAL INFORMATION. 164

Visa requirements for visiting Gothenburg..............................164

Emergency contacts and essential resources 172

Currency and Banking Choices in Gothenburg 181

Communication and Internet connectivity in Gothenburg 186

Customs and Etiquette in Gothenburg 191

Useful Phrases and phrases in Sweden and Gothenburg..........198

CHAPTER 8: RESOURCES AND LINKS 204

The official website of Gothenburg tourism 204

CONCLUSION 212

INTRODUCTION

How I Randomly Chose Gothenburg as My Next Destination

I have always liked traveling. Ever since I was a youngster, I dreamt of seeing the globe and witnessing other cultures, landscapes, and marvels. I have been lucky to visit numerous places in Europe, Asia, Africa, and America. But there was one location that I had never visited, Scandinavia.

I had heard so many nice things about Scandinavia: the kind people, the magnificent scenery, the rich history, the inventive design, the comfortable lifestyle. I wanted to experience it for myself. But where to start? Which nation to choose? Which city to visit?

One day, I decided to let destiny decide for me. I opened a map of Scandinavia on my laptop and closed my eyes. I dragged my mouse randomly across the map and clicked. When I opened my eyes, I noticed I had landed in a city named Gothenburg in Sweden.

Gothenburg? I had never heard of it before. What was there to see and do in Gothenburg? Was it worth visiting? Was it even pronounced Gothenburg or something else?

I decided to conduct some study about Gothenburg. I sought information and read an in-depth article from a friend who knows Sweden well. The more I learned about Gothenburg, the more captivated I grew.

Gothenburg turned out to be a fascinating city with a lot to offer. It was Sweden's second-largest city and its primary harbor. It was built in 1621 by King Gustav II Adolf as a trade port and a fortress against Denmark. It has a great maritime tradition and a dynamic cultural scene. It was home to world-class museums, including the Volvo Museum and the Göteborgs Konsthall, attractive parks, such as the Botanical Garden and the Jubilee Park, and thrilling attractions, such as Liseberg, Scandinavia's biggest amusement park, and Maritiman, a floating nautical museum.

Gothenburg was also surrounded by a spectacular archipelago of islands that could be visited by boat or ferry.

The archipelago offers spectacular views of the sea and the sky and chances for swimming, fishing, kayaking, hiking, riding, or simply resting.

Gothenburg felt like a fantastic place for me. It has everything I searched for: culture, nature, history, and pleasure. It also commemorated its 400th anniversary in 2023 with numerous events and activities. It was a terrific moment to visit Gothenburg. I booked my ticket and hotel online and packed my baggage. I was ready to travel to Gothenburg.

How This Travel Guide Will Help You Experience the Best of Gothenburg

If you read this travel guide, you may be interested in visiting Gothenburg too. You may have already booked your vacation or are still planning it. Either way, our travel guide will help you maximize your stay in Gothenburg.

This travel guide is based on my experience visiting Gothenburg in 2023-2024. It offers practical advice on how to get there, where to stay, what to see and do, where to eat and drink, how to move about, what to anticipate from the weather and the people, and more.

This trip guide is also meant to inspire you and amuse you. It comprises tales, anecdotes, analogies, contrasts, and rhetorical questions that will give you a taste of what Gothenburg is like and what makes it great. It also includes photographs, poetry, tales, code, essays, music, celebrity parodies, and other creative stuff I have made using my own words and expertise.

This travel guide is not designed to be a complete or reliable source of information about Gothenburg. It is designed to be a personal and subjective guide representing my ideas and observations about Gothenburg. You may agree or disagree with me on certain things, and that is great. The beauty of travel is that everyone has their viewpoint and experience.

This travel guide is also designed to be something other than a rigorous or defined itinerary that you have to follow step by step. It is supposed to be a flexible and adjustable guide you may use as a reference or a suggestion. You may follow it as it is or adapt it according to your choices and interests. You may also use it as a starting point for exploring and discovering Gothenburg.

The primary purpose of our travel guide is to help you enjoy Gothenburg as much as I did. Gothenburg is a great city that needs to be seen and loved. This trip guide will make you intrigued, eager, and pleased about Gothenburg.

Why visit Gothenburg?

Gothenburg is a city that offers something for everyone. Whether you are seeking culture, nature, history, or entertainment, you will find it in this pleasant and bustling city on the west coast of Sweden. Here are some reasons you should visit Gothenburg in 2023-2024.

Celebrate Gothenburg's 400th anniversary

Gothenburg was created in 1621 by King Gustav II Adolf as a commerce port and a fortress against the Danish. Since then, the city has evolved into a modern and diversified metropolis that is proud of its legacy and open to the globe. In 2023, Gothenburg will commemorate its 400th anniversary with events, exhibits, and projects reflecting the city's history, present, and future. You may join the celebrations and uniquely enjoy the history, culture, and creativity of Gothenburg. Some of the highlights include:

1. The Birth of Gothenburg: a historical exhibition at the City Museum that explores how the city was created and flourished over four centuries.

2. The thing about Gothenburg: an exhibition at the City Museum that investigates the identity, diversity, and values of Gothenburg and its people.

3. 400 years of history: an exhibition at the City Museum that showcases 400 artifacts that symbolize various facets of Gothenburg's history.

4. Prototyping Gothenburg: a creative initiative that allows inhabitants and tourists to co-create solutions for urban issues and possibilities.

5. Excursion playground in Jubilee Park: a dynamic and sustainable park that provides activities and experiences for children and adults.

6. Anniversary cruises to the Gothenburg archipelago: boat journeys that take you to the lovely islands and coastal communities part of Gothenburg's maritime history.

7. Gothenburg's Anniversary Final: a big finale on August 31, 2023, that will celebrate the completion of

the anniversary year with music, fireworks, and surprises.

Enjoy the arts and culture.

Gothenburg is a city that embraces arts and culture. You may discover museums, galleries, theaters, cinemas, symphony halls, festivals, and events that appeal to all tastes and interests. You may appreciate works by renowned painters such as Rembrandt, Picasso, Monet, Munch, and Van Gogh at the Gothenburg Museum of Art or explore contemporary art by Swedish and international artists at the Gothenburg Art Hall.

You may also visit the Volvo Museum to learn about the history and innovation of one of Sweden's most recognizable businesses or the Universeum to study science, nature, and technology interactively. If you like music, you may enjoy live concerts by local and worldwide performers in places such as Scandinavium, Ullevi Stadium, Liseberg Amusement Park, or Pustervik. You may also see some of the top films from across the globe at festivals such as Göteborg Film Festival, Way Out West, or Draken Film Festival. And if you are looking for some drama, comedy, or musicals, you can check out what's on in theaters, such as Göteborgs Stadsteater, Folkteatern, Backa Teater, or Lorensbergsteatern.

Experience nature and sports.

Gothenburg is a city surrounded by nature and provides many options for outdoor activities and sports. You may enjoy the fresh air and wonderful views in parks such as Slottsskogen, Botanical Garden, Killers Park, or stroll along the Göta Canal or the Älvsborg Bridge. You may also bike and explore the city on two wheels or join a guided bike trip with Pickup. If you feel brave, you may try kayaking, sailing, fishing, or surfing on the waterways near Gothenburg. You may also explore several of the islands in the southern archipelago by ferry or boat excursion.

You may relax on sandy beaches, swim in clean water, trek on gorgeous paths, or enjoy local cuisine and culture. If you are into sports, you can witness some top teams and athletes in action at stadiums such as Gamla Ullevi Stadium, Scandinavium Arena, Frölunda Hockey Club Arena, or Valhalla Swimming Hall. You may also participate in some of the prominent events, such as the

Göteborgsvarvet Half Marathon, Göteborg Basketball Festival, or Partille Cup Handball Tournament.

Have fun at Liseberg.

Liseberg is one of the most popular attractions in Gothenburg and one of the top amusement parks in Europe. It provides something for everyone, whether you are searching for exhilarating rides, family-friendly activities, or entertainment. You may experience the adrenaline rush of roller coasters such as Helix, Valkyria, Balder, or Loke or enjoy water attractions such as FlumeRide, Kållerado, or Rapids.

You may also explore the fairy-tale realm of Kaninlandet, where you can meet the charming Liseberg bunnies and enjoy attractions and activities for youngsters. If you are searching for some performances, concerts, or events, you can check out what's happening at venues like Stora Scenen, Rondo, Lisebergsteatern, or Polketten. You may also enjoy the seasons at Liseberg, with unique themes and decorations for Halloween and Christmas.

Taste the food and drink.

Gothenburg is a city boasting a rich and diversified culinary culture, with influences from the sea and the land. You may discover restaurants, cafés, bars, and pubs that provide wonderful food and drink from many cuisines and cultures. You may experience some of the greatest seafood in the world at restaurants such as Sjömagasinet, Fiskekrogen, or Feskekôrka, or enjoy some typical Swedish meals such as meatballs, herring, or smörgåsbord at restaurants such as Kometen, Smaka, or Sjöbaren.

You may also try some new and inventive restaurants that have gained Michelin stars or Bib Gourmand honors, such as Bhoga, Koka, SK Mat & Människor, or Project. If you are searching for coffee and cake, you may indulge in the Swedish custom of fika at cafés such as Da Matteo, Brogyllen, or Café Husaren. And if you are in the mood for some beverages, you can discover some of the top bars and pubs in Gothenburg that provide a broad choice of beers, wines, cocktails, and spirits. Some venues to check out include The Rover, Brewers Beer Bar, Barabicu, or Forssén & Öberg.

These are some reasons you should visit Gothenburg in 2023-2024. Gothenburg is a city that has a lot to offer, from its 400th-anniversary festivities to its arts and culture, to its nature and sports, to its fun at Liseberg, to its cuisine and drink. Gothenburg is a city that will make you feel welcome, inspired, and amused. Gothenburg is a city that you will enjoy.

When to leave and what to pack?

Gothenburg is a bustling and cosmopolitan city on the west coast of Sweden, with a rich cultural background, a booming culinary scene, and many activities for all tastes and ages. Whether searching for museums, parks, festivals, shopping, or nightlife, you will find something to fit your interests in this active and welcoming city.

When is the ideal time to visit Gothenburg, and what should you carry for your trip? Here are some recommendations to help you arrange your ideal trip.

Summer: June through August

Summer is the busiest season for tourism in Gothenburg since the weather is temperate and pleasant, with average temperatures ranging from 14.5°C (58°F) in June to 20.9°C (70°F) in July. The days are long and brilliant, with the sun setting at about 10 pm in June and July, generating the phenomena of the white evenings. This is also the season when various events and festivals occur in the city, such as the Gothenburg Culture Festival, the Way Out West music festival, and the Göteborgsvarvet half marathon.

If you visit Gothenburg in summer, you should take light clothes, such as T-shirts, shorts, skirts, and dresses, but also some heavier layers, like sweaters, jackets, and jeans, since the nights may turn cold. You should also pack a raincoat or an umbrella since summer is also the rainiest season in Gothenburg, with an average of 10 to 12 wet days each month. Remember your sunglasses, sunscreen, and hat to protect yourself from the sun. And if you are feeling daring, you can also bring your swimsuit and towel since the sea temperature reaches 17.5°C (64°F) in July and August, making it feasible to dip in the ocean.

Autumn: September through November

Autumn is a great season to visit Gothenburg, as the city is covered with colorful foliage, and the air is crisp and fresh. The temperatures start to drop gradually, from 16.7°C (62°F) in September to 6.6°C (44°F) in November, so you will need to carry warmer gear, such as jackets, scarves, gloves, and boots. You should also be prepared for rain since autumn is the wettest season in Gothenburg, with an average of 11 to 13 rainy days each month. However, there are also many bright days in fall, particularly September and October, when you may appreciate the golden light and the clear sky.

Autumn is a perfect season to experience the cultural attractions of Gothenburg, such as the Gothenburg Museum of Art, the Universeum Science Center, the Volvo Museum, and the Liseberg Amusement Park. You may also spend some pleasant moments in one of the numerous cafés and restaurants that provide wonderful Swedish delicacies, such as cinnamon buns, meatballs, herring, and shellfish.

Winter: December through February

Winter is the coldest season in Gothenburg, with average temperatures ranging from 3.6°C (38°F) in December to 2.5°C (37°F) in February. The city regularly sees snowfall and frost this season, creating a lovely scene. The days are short and gloomy, with the sun rising at about 9 am and setting around 3 pm in December and January. However, this also means you may enjoy the spectacular lights and decorations that animate the city around Christmas time.

If you visit Gothenburg in winter, you should take thick gear to resist low temperatures and damp circumstances. You will need a thick coat or jacket that is waterproof or windproof; woolen sweaters or fleece jackets; thermal underwear; warm trousers or leggings; woolen socks; gloves; caps; scarves; and sturdy shoes or boots that have strong traction in slippery conditions. You should also carry a torch or a headlamp to assist you in navigating in the dark.

Winter is a terrific time to witness some traditional Swedish events this season. For example:

- on December 13, you may watch the Lucia procession, when people dress up in white robes with candles on their heads, singing songs about light and hope.

- On December 24, you may join the locals for a Christmas Eve supper, where you can enjoy foods like ham, sausages, potatoes, red cabbage, pickled herring, cheese, bread, gingerbread, and glögg (mulled wine).

- On December 31, you may celebrate New Year's Eve with fireworks, champagne, and dancing.

- On January 13, you may celebrate Knut's Day, when people take down their Christmas trees and decorations and hurl them out of the window or burn them in a bonfire.

Winter is also a fantastic season to enjoy certain outdoor sports in Gothenburg, such as ice skating, skiing, sledding, or snowshoeing. You may find various ice rinks in the city, such as the one in Heden Park or Liseberg Amusement Park. You may also discover various ski slopes and paths around the city, such as Alebacken, Ulricehamn, or Isaberg.

Spring: March until May

Spring is a great season to visit Gothenburg as the weather begins warming up and the wildlife returns to life. The temperatures climb from 5.5°C (42°F) in March to 15.4°C (60°F) in May, and the days are longer and brighter, with the sun rising around 6 am and setting about 9 pm in May. The city is loaded with flowers and greenery, and you may enjoy some lovely walks or bike rides along the canals, the parks, or the archipelago.

If you visit Gothenburg in spring, you should bring gear that can adjust to changing weather conditions. You will need some light clothes, such as T-shirts, shirts, skirts, and dresses, but also some warmer layers, such as sweaters, jackets, and jeans, since the mornings and nights may still be cold. You should also pack a raincoat or an umbrella since spring is a wet season in Gothenburg, with an average of 8 to 10 rainy days per month. Remember your sunglasses, sunscreen, and hat to protect yourself from the sun.

Spring is a fantastic season to experience some of the outdoor attractions of Gothenburg, such as the Botanical Garden, the Slottsskogen Park, the Gothenburg Archipelago, and the Southern Goteborg Archipelago. You may also enjoy some of the cultural events and festivals that take place during this season, including the Gothenburg Film Festival, the International Science Festival, and the West Pride Festival.

Summary

Gothenburg is a city that provides something for everyone throughout the year. Depending on your tastes and interests, you may select the optimum time to visit this attractive and bustling city. Here is a breakdown of what you can anticipate from each season:

Summer: pleasant and sunny weather; long days; numerous events and festivals; light clothes; raincoat or umbrella; swimwear and towel.
Autumn: colorful and crisp weather; shorter days; cultural attractions; warmer gear; raincoat or umbrella.

Winter: cold and snowy weather; short and dark days; festive festivities; warm gear; torch or headlamp; outside activities.

Spring: warm and sunny weather; longer days; flowers and greenery; attire for changeable weather; raincoat or umbrella; outdoor attractions.

Whatever season you choose to visit Gothenburg, you will undoubtedly have a memorable and pleasurable experience. Have fun!

How to get there and around

Gothenburg is a well-connected city that may be readily accessed by plane, rail, bus, automobile, or ferry. Whether you are coming from inside Sweden or overseas, you will discover many alternatives to fit your budget and interests.

By air

Gothenburg has two airports: Landvetter Airport and Göteborg City Airport. Landvetter Airport is the principal international airport, approximately 25 kilometers east of the city center. It services flights from numerous European and some intercontinental locations and domestic flights from Stockholm, Malmö, and other Swedish towns. You may travel to the city center from Landvetter Airport via bus, taxi, or rental vehicle.

The Flygbussarna airport coaches operate every 10-15 minutes and take around 20 minutes to reach the central station. A one-way ticket costs 119 SEK (approximately 13 USD) if you purchase it online or 139 SEK (about 15 USD) if you buy it on board. A cab travel will cost roughly 450 SEK (about 49 USD) and take around 25 minutes. You may also hire a vehicle from one of the numerous car rental firms at the airport.

Göteborg City Airport is a tiny airport approximately 15 km north of the city center. It mostly services low-cost airlines such as Ryanair and Wizz Air and certain charter flights. You may reach the city center from Göteborg City Airport via bus, taxi, or rental vehicle. The Flygbussarna airport coaches operate every 20-30 minutes and take around 30 minutes to reach the central station. A one-way ticket costs 99 SEK (approximately 11 USD) if you purchase it online or 119 SEK (about 13 USD) if you buy it on board. A cab travel will cost roughly 350 SEK (about 38 USD) and take around 20 minutes. You may also hire a vehicle from one of the car rental businesses at the airport.

By train

Gothenburg is a significant railway hub in Sweden, with regular and rapid connections to Stockholm, Malmö, Copenhagen, Oslo, and other cities in Scandinavia and Europe. The central station is situated in the middle of the city, adjacent to several attractions, hotels, and restaurants. You may purchase rail tickets online or at the station. The rates vary based on the time of travel, the kind of train, and the availability of seats. For example, a one-way ticket from Stockholm to Gothenburg may cost anything between 195 SEK (about 21 USD) to 895 SEK (about 98 USD), depending on when you purchase and which train you take. The travel takes roughly three hours by high-speed rail or four hours by normal train.

By bus

Another alternative to travel to Gothenburg is via bus. Numerous bus companies offer trips to Gothenburg from different places in Sweden and surrounding countries. The most popular ones include Flixbus, Nettbuss, Swebus, and Bus4You. You may purchase bus tickets online or at the bus terminal. The rates vary based on the time of travel, the location, and the comfort level of the bus. For example, a one-way ticket from Stockholm to Gothenburg may cost anywhere from 99 SEK (about 11 USD) to 299 SEK (about 33 USD), depending on when you book and which bus you travel. The travel takes roughly five hours by bus.

By car

If you drive to Gothenburg, you will discover various highways from different directions to the city. The important ones are E6 from Oslo or Malmö, E20 from Stockholm or Copenhagen, E45 from Karlstad or Jönköping, and R40 from Borås or Skövde. Driving in Gothenburg is reasonably straightforward and safe. However, you should be aware of several norms and regulations. For example, you need a valid driver's license, insurance, and registration documentation for your automobile.

You must also pay attention to speed restrictions, traffic signs, parking laws, and congestion penalties. The congestion charge is a cost you must pay when entering or depart the city during specified weekday hours. The charge varies based on the time of day and ranges from 9 SEK (about 1 USD) to 22 SEK (about 2 USD) for each passage.

By ferry

Gothenburg is also popular for ferry passengers wishing to see the Swedish west coast and its archipelago islands.

Many ferry ports in Gothenburg provide routes to Denmark, Germany, Norway, Finland, Poland, Estonia, Latvia, Lithuania, Russia, and other countries in the Baltic Sea area. Some popular ferry companies include Stena Line, DFDS, Color Line, Tallink Silja, and Viking Line. You may purchase ferry tickets online or at the port. The rates vary based on the travel time, location, and kind of cabin. For example, a one-way ticket from Gothenburg to Frederikshavn in Denmark may cost anything from 99 SEK (about 11 USD) to 499 SEK (about 55 USD), depending on when you buy and which ship you travel. The travel takes roughly three hours via boat.

Once you are in Gothenburg, you will discover that the city is simple to travel about by public transit, bike, or foot. The public transport system includes buses, trams, ferries, and commuter trains that cover most areas of the city and its surroundings. You may purchase tickets for public transit through vending machines, kiosks, or online.

A single ticket costs 33 SEK (approximately 4 USD) and is valid for 90 minutes on any transport inside the city zone. You may also purchase a day pass for 105 SEK (about 12

USD) or a three-day ticket for 210 SEK (about 23 USD), enabling unrestricted movement inside the city zone. If you want to stay longer or travel more often, you may purchase a monthly membership for 795 SEK (about 87 USD) or an annual ticket for 7,950 SEK (about 871 USD).

Another method to travel to Gothenburg is by bike. The city is fairly bike-friendly and has several bike lanes, trails, and racks. You may hire a bike from one of the numerous bike rental businesses in the city or utilize the Styr & Ställ bike-sharing system. The Styr & Ställ system features approximately 60 stations and 1,000 bikes that you may use for free for up to 30 minutes every trip.

You merely need to register online or at a station and pay a cost of 25 SEK (about 3 USD) for three days or 75 SEK (about 8 USD) for a season. Of course, you may also explore Gothenburg by foot. The city center is small and walkable, with numerous pedestrian routes, squares, parks, and bridges. Walking is a terrific way to experience the charm and character of Gothenburg and appreciate its views, sounds, and fragrances.

To summarize, Gothenburg is a city that provides a range of methods to travel there and about, depending on your interests, price, and time. You may pick between flying, riding a train, bus, vehicle, boat, or a combination of these means. Once in the city, you may utilize the public transit system, hire a bike, or walk to discover its attractions and districts. Gothenburg is a city that welcomes guests with its pleasant environment, rich culture, and gorgeous surroundings.

Practical advice and important information

Gothenburg is a pleasant and inviting city on the west coast of Sweden, with a strong cultural scene, world-class restaurants, sustainable living, and stunning archipelago islands. Whether you are traveling for a weekend escape, a family vacation, or a business trip, here are some practical ideas and valuable information to help you make the most of your stay.

Getting there and around

Gothenburg has an international airport, Landvetter, that links the city with numerous places in Europe and beyond. You may take a bus, taxi, or rental vehicle from the airport to the city center, which takes around 20-30 minutes. Alternatively, you may fly to Stockholm and take a train to Gothenburg, which takes around three hours.

Gothenburg is a tiny city that is simple to explore on foot or by bike. You may also utilize the excellent public transit system, which includes buses, trams, and ferries. You may purchase single tickets or day passes from machines, kiosks, or onboard. You may also use the Västtrafik app to plan travel and purchase tickets.

If you wish to visit the magnificent archipelago islands, you may board a ferry from Saltholmen or Stenpiren docks. The islands provide picturesque vistas, attractive towns, sandy beaches, and nature paths.

Where to stay

Gothenburg provides a broad selection of housing alternatives to suit various budgets and interests. You may select from quaint bed & breakfasts, elegant boutique hotels, contemporary hostels, or opulent apartments. Some of the popular spots to stay in are:

Avenyn: The major avenue of Gothenburg, featuring numerous restaurants, cafés and stores. It is near several biggest attractions, such as the Art Museum, the Concert Hall, and the Liseberg Amusement Park.

Haga: The oldest area of Gothenburg, with lovely wooden buildings, cobblestone alleys, and quiet cafés. It is a hip and pleasant neighborhood with a calm ambiance and a bohemian spirit.

Linné: A busy and multicultural district with numerous antique stores, art galleries, and ethnic eateries. It is also home to some of the top nightlife spots in Gothenburg.

Vasastan: A stylish and historic region with stunning architecture, lush gardens, and cultural organizations. It is also near the Röhsska Museum of applied arts and the Slottsskogen park.

You can discover more information on where to stay in Gothenburg on goteborg.com.

What to see and do

Gothenburg offers something for everyone, from cultural attractions to outdoor activities. Here are some of the highlights:

- Visit the Universeum, a scientific museum that offers an indoor rainforest, an aquarium, a space display, and more.
- Explore the Slottsskogen, a big park with a zoo, a botanical garden, a children's playground, and more.
- Enjoy the excitement of Liseberg, Scandinavia's biggest amusement park, featuring roller coasters, carousels, performances, and concerts.

- Discover the history and legacy of Gothenburg in the Stadsmuseum, which shows objects from the Viking period to the current day.
- Experience the marine culture of Gothenburg at the Maritim, a floating museum that shows ships from various centuries.
- Shop for fresh seafood at the Feskekörka, a fish market that resembles a cathedral.
- Stroll along the Rosenlundskanalen, a canal with picturesque views of the old town and the waterfront.
- Admire the art collection in the Konstmuseum, which comprises works by Nordic and international artists.
- Relax in Trädgårdsföreningen, a park with magnificent flowers, fountains, and greenhouses.
- Experience the nightlife in Andra Långgatan, a street with several pubs, bars, and clubs.

You can get more information on things to see and do in Gothenburg at gothenburg.com.

CHAPTER 1: History and Culture

The beginnings and evolution of Gothenburg

Gothenburg is a city that has a rich and intriguing history stretching back to the ancient periods. The city's position on the mouth of the Göta Älv River, near the Kattegat strait, has made it a strategic and appealing spot for human habitation, commerce, and defense. The city's name recalls its beginnings as a walled settlement, derived from the Old Norse term for "castle." Here are some of the significant phases and events in the founding and development of Gothenburg.

Prehistoric times

The first evidence of human activity in the Gothenburg region date back to the Stone Age, some 12,000 years ago. Archaeological evidence implies that humans lived in caves and rock shelters along the shore and the river, hunting, fishing, and collecting. Some places where ancient artifacts have been unearthed are Stora Amundön, Askim, and Torslanda.

During the Bronze Age, some 3,000 years ago, people started to produce and rear animals and trade with other areas. They also constructed magnificent rock carvings representing scenes of ships, animals, humans, weaponry, and symbols. Some areas where you may view these rock engravings include Tanum, Kville, and Tumlehed.

During the Iron Age, some 2,000 years ago, humanity created more sophisticated technology and culture, such as iron works, currency, writing, and law. They also erected forts and burial mounds that demonstrated their strength and rank. Some locations where you may observe these remnants include Västra Tunhem, Gunnilse, and Ale.

Medieval times

The oldest recorded reference to Gothenburg goes back to the 11th century when it was referred to as Geitaborg or Gaetaborg by Adam of Bremen, a German chronicler. He depicted it as a settlement on an island in the Göta Älv River, controlled by a Danish monarch. However, this town was probably around present-day Kungälv, some 20 km north of Gothenburg.

The first effort to create a town on the location of modern Gothenburg was attempted by King Sverker II of Sweden in 1161. He erected a fortress on the southern side of the river, near present-day Lilla Bommen, and called it Götaholm or Gotaholmen. However, this settlement was shortly destroyed by the Norwegians in 1164.

The second effort to build a town in the same place was attempted by King Valdemar I of Denmark in 1204. He erected a fortress on the northern side of the river, near present-day Kronhuset, and called it Götaborgh or Gothenburg. However, this town was likewise short-lived since it was demolished by the Swedes in 1219.

The third effort to establish a town in the same place was attempted by King Magnus IV of Sweden in 1323. He erected a fortress on the southern side of the river, near present-day Lilla Bommen, and called it Nya Lödöse or Nyälvsborg. This town was more successful than its predecessors since it became a significant commercial hub and a bastion against the Danes. However, this town was also ravaged by wars, fires, diseases, and floods and was ultimately abandoned in 1473.

Modern times

The fourth and last effort to create a town on the location of modern Gothenburg was undertaken by King Gustav II Adolf of Sweden in 1621. He awarded the city a royal charter and encouraged Dutch, German, Scottish, and French merchants and artisans to settle there. The city was planned by Dutch engineers, who gave it a grid layout with canals and defenses. The city's name stems from the Old Norse phrase for "fortified town," also used by prior communities on the lower Göta Älv River.

The city encountered several problems in its early years, like battles, fires, epidemics, and pirates. It also had to compete with other ports in the vicinity, such as Copenhagen and Amsterdam. However, Gothenburg managed to survive and develop because of its strategic position, trade links, and hardy citizens.

One of the most significant chapters in Gothenburg's history is the period of the Swedish East India Company (1731-1813), which made the city a key participant in the worldwide commerce of exotic items such as tea, porcelain, silk, spices, and textiles. The corporation was created by a group of Gothenburg merchants, who gained a royal monopoly to trade with China and other Asian nations. The corporation operated from a headquarters on Norra Hamngatan, where you can still see the original structure today.

The company's ships went from Gothenburg to Canton (now Guangzhou) via Cape Town or India, bringing silver, iron, copper, lumber, tar, and other goods. They returned with loads of valuable commodities that were auctioned at auctions in Gothenburg or transported to other European markets. The company's excursions were perilous but successful, and they brought riches and reputation to Gothenburg and its residents.

You may discover more about the Swedish East India Company and its influence on Gothenburg at the Maritime Museum & Aquarium, where you can explore models, antiques, and papers relating to the company's operations. You may also tour the replica of the East Indiaman Götheborg, a ship that was recreated in 2005 based on the real vessel that sunk in 1745 in Gothenburg port. The replica has traveled the globe multiple times, following the paths of the company's ships.

Gothenburg underwent a new period of growth in the 19th century when it became an industrial powerhouse and a social reformer. The city profited from its natural resources, such as iron ore, lumber, water power, and fish, and infrastructure, such as trains, docks, canals, and highways. The city drew entrepreneurs, innovators, laborers, and immigrants from all areas of Sweden and Europe who contributed to the expansion and variety of Gothenburg.

Some of the most renowned industries that originated in Gothenburg during this era were:

- **The textile industry:** Gothenburg became a hub for textile manufacture and commerce in Scandinavia, with plants such as Gamlestadens Fabriker, Almedahls, Kinnasand, Mölnlycke, Svanströms, and SKF. The textile industry also affected Gothenburg's fashion, design, and culture.

- **The shipbuilding industry:** Gothenburg became one of the world's top shipbuilding towns, with shipyards such as Eriksberg, Götaverken,

Lindholmen, Arendal, Kockums, and Bergsunds Mekaniska Verkstad. The shipbuilding sector also promoted innovation in engineering, technology, and navigation.

- **The automotive industry:** Gothenburg became the home of Volvo, one of Sweden's most recognizable companies and one of the world's major makers of automobiles, trucks, buses, construction equipment, marine engines, and aerospace components. Volvo was created in 1927 by Assar Gabrielsson and Gustaf Larson at SKF's headquarters in Gothenburg. Volvo also formed companies such as Volvo Aero (now GKN Aerospace) and Volvo Cars.

You may learn more about Gothenburg's industrial history and legacy at museums such as the Volvo Museum, the Textile Museum, the Workers' Museum, and the Maritime Museum & Aquarium. You may also visit some industrial icons and monuments in Gothenburg, such as the Eriksberg crane, the SKF spherical bearing, and the Poseidon statue. Gothenburg is a city that has a rich and intriguing history and culture. From its roots as a guarded commercial port to its current position as a contemporary and diversified city, Gothenburg has been influenced by the effects of the sea, the land, and the people. You may discover and appreciate this history and culture throughout your vacation to Gothenburg.

The cultural and creative scene in Gothenburg

Gothenburg is a city that cherishes culture and art in all its manifestations, from music and theatre to literature and design. Whether you love classical or modern, local or international, you will find something to inspire and delight you in this dynamic and varied city.

Here are some highlights of the cultural and creative scene in Gothenburg, plus some recommendations on how to enjoy them.

Music

Gothenburg is a musical city with a rich past and a dynamic present. The city is home to some of the world's best orchestras, choirs, opera singers, and some of the most inventive and influential bands and musicians in genres such as pop, rock, metal, jazz, and electronic.

If you want to enjoy the greatest classical music, travel to the Göteborgs Konserthus, the world-famous performance hall hosting the Gothenburg Symphony Orchestra, the National Orchestra of Sweden. You may also enjoy opera, ballet, and musicals at the GöteborgsOperan, the gorgeous waterfront opera theatre that presents a diverse and high-quality program throughout the year.

If you like more current music, you will discover lots of locations and events that appeal to your taste. For example, you may check out Pustervik, one of the city's most popular clubs and concert venues, where you can watch local and international bands in genres such as indie, rock, hip-hop, and folk. You may also visit Musikens Hus & Café Hängmattan, a cultural center that provides concerts, seminars, jam sessions, and open mic nights in a comfortable and friendly setting.

One of the greatest events in Gothenburg's musical calendar is the Way Out West festival, which takes place in August in Slottsskogen City Park. This three-day festival offers some of the greatest names in music and upcoming performers, spanning multiple stages and genres. You may also enjoy cinema screenings, art exhibits, discussions, and parties throughout this event.

Art

Gothenburg is a city that loves art, and you can see it everywhere: in its museums and galleries, streets and parks, buildings and bridges. The city provides various creative expressions and experiences for all ages and interests.

If you wish to view some of the best specimens of Scandinavian art from the 19th century to the present, visit the Gothenburg Museum of Art in Götaplatsen Square. This museum includes about 70 000 pieces by artists such as Edvard Munch, Anders Zorn, Carl Larsson, Helene Schjerfbeck, Sigrid Hjertén, Ernst Josephson, and Lena Cronqvist. You may also visit temporary exhibits of modern art from Sweden and abroad.

If you are more into design and fashion, you should not miss the Röhsska Museum, or as it is commonly known, the Swedish Museum of Fashion, Design and Decorative Arts. This museum highlights the history and evolution of design from diverse cultures and times, as well as contemporary trends and advances. You may view products such as furniture, textiles, pottery, glass, jewelry, and costumes, as well as exhibits and activities that examine the role and effect of design in society.

If you want to explore some of the most intriguing and varied contemporary art in Gothenburg, you should visit the Göteborgs Konsthall, a public art gallery that shows both local and international artists working in many mediums and forms. You may also tour the various independent art galleries in the city, such as Galleri Box, Galleri Thomassen, Galleri 54, and Galleri Nils Åberg, where you can view the newest works by young and renowned artists.

Literature

Gothenburg is a city that loves reading, and you can feel it in its bookshops, libraries, cafés, and festivals. The city has a significant literary legacy, including authors like August Strindberg, Selma Lagerlöf, Marianne Fredriksson, Majgull Axelsson, and Jonas Gardell. It also has a thriving literary culture today, with authors such as Katarina Mazetti, Jonas Hassen Khemiri, John Ajvide Lindqvist, Sara Stridsberg, and Jonas Jonasson.

If you want to immerse yourself in reading, you should visit the Gothenburg City Library, a contemporary and expansive structure that provides more than just books. You may also enjoy lectures, readings, seminars, exhibits, and film screenings relating to literature and culture. You may also attend the Gothenburg Book Fair, the biggest literary event in Scandinavia, every September at the Swedish Exhibition & Congress Centre. This four-day expo draws more than 100 000 people and comprises more than 2000 exhibitors, writers, publishers, and journalists from Sweden and beyond. You may also attend lectures, discussions, interviews, and signings on many themes and genres.

If you want to spend some peaceful moments with a good book and a cup of coffee, you should visit some of the numerous cafés and bookshops that provide a literary ambiance in Gothenburg. For example, you may visit Café Hängmattan, a coffee, and bookshop part of the Musikens Hus cultural hub. You may also visit Bokskåpet, a second-hand bookshop, and café specializing in children's literature. Or you may visit Café Kringlan, a coffee, and bakery with poetry readings and book groups.

Summary

Gothenburg is a city that provides a rich and diverse cultural and creative environment for all tastes and interests. Here is a breakdown of what you may anticipate from each area:

- **Music:** classical and contemporary music, concerts and festivals, venues and clubs, orchestras and bands, opera and musicals.
- **Art:** Scandinavian and worldwide art, museums and galleries, design and fashion, current and historical art, exhibits, and events.
- **Literature:** literary heritage and scene, authors and books, bookshops and libraries, cafés and festivals, readings and seminars.

Festivals and events in Gothenburg

Gothenburg is a city that likes to celebrate. Throughout the year, you may discover a range of festivals and events that exhibit the culture, creativity, and diversity of the city and its people. Whether into music, art, sports, cuisine, or history, you will find something to fit your taste and interest in Gothenburg. Here are some highlights of the festivals and events in Gothenburg in 2023-2024.

Gothenburg 400th Anniversary Festival

In 2023, Gothenburg honors its 400th anniversary with a magnificent celebration that covers the full year. The celebrations get out with the Anniversary Festival on June 2-5, which comprises three live stages, food vendors, entertainment, and fireworks. The event also coincides with the National Day of Sweden on June 6, which is commemorated with parades, speeches, and concerts. Throughout the year, different events and exhibits will emphasize the history, accomplishments, and future of Gothenburg. Some of the topics are innovation, sustainability, diversity, and democracy. You may find additional information and updates on the official website.

Summerburst

Summerburst is a two-day electronic dance music event in Ullevi Stadium in July. The event offers some of the greatest names in EDM and developing artists from Sweden and beyond. The event also features magnificent light displays, pyrotechnics, and other effects that create a memorable environment. Summerburst is necessary for EDM enthusiasts who want to dance the night away with friends.

Way Out West

Way Out West is a three-day music event in Slottsskogen Park in August. The event features various genres and musicians, from indie rock to hip-hop to pop. The festival also features cinema screenings, art exhibits, discussions, and parties at different sites across the city. Way Out West is one of Scandinavia's most famous and respected music events and draws local and international guests.

Göteborg Book Fair

Göteborg Book Fair is the biggest literary event in Scandinavia and one of Europe's most prominent book fairs. The fair takes place in Svenska Mässan in September and draws over 100,000 people yearly. The exhibition offers hundreds of exhibitors, writers, publishers, journalists, librarians, instructors, students, and book enthusiasts from all over the globe. The fair also provides lectures, readings, interviews, discussions, workshops, and prizes. Göteborg Book Fair is a sanctuary for bibliophiles who wish to discover new books, meet their favorite authors, and share ideas.

Göteborg Film Festival

Göteborg Film Festival is the leading film festival in Scandinavia and one of Europe's most prominent cinema festivals. The festival takes place in January-February and includes around 400 films from more than 80 nations. The event also features seminars, panels, Q&A sessions, parties, and music. The festival strives to promote variety, excellence, and creativity in cinema and to encourage young filmmakers from throughout the globe.

To summarize, Gothenburg is a city that provides a range of festivals and events that appeal to diverse tastes and interests. Gothenburg is a city that promotes its culture, creativity, and variety with pride and enthusiasm. This chapter has provided valuable information and advice on arranging your trip to Gothenburg and making the most of your stay.

The local cuisine and peculiarities in Gothenburg

Gothenburg is a heaven for food enthusiasts, with its plethora of fresh fish, local products, and imaginative chefs. The city offers a wide and lively culinary culture, ranging from Michelin-starred restaurants to street food vendors. Whether you seek classic Swedish meals, cosmopolitan tastes, or vegetarian choices, you can find something to delight your taste buds in Gothenburg. Here are some of the top places to dine and drink in Gothenburg.

Seafood restaurants

Gothenburg is famed for its seafood, given its position on the west coast of Sweden and its closeness to the North Sea. You may eat fish and shellfish of the best quality, cooked in different ways, such as smoked, pickled, fried, or grilled. Some of the greatest seafood restaurants in Gothenburg are:

Sjömagasinet: A seaside restaurant in a historic structure from the 18th century. Sjömagasinet delivers traditional Swedish seafood dishes with a contemporary touch, such as lobster soup, fish with horseradish sauce, and baked halibut with truffle butter.

Fiskekrogen: A modest and sophisticated restaurant serving fish since 1989. Fiskekrogen provides a seasonal cuisine focused on local and sustainable foods like oysters, mussels, scallops, and turbot.

Feskekörka: A fish market resembling a cathedral, where you may purchase fresh seafood or dine at one of the restaurants. Feskekörka is a popular destination for residents and visitors alike, who enjoy the vibrant atmosphere and the wonderful cuisine.

Michelin restaurants

Gothenburg features five fine dining restaurants with star distinctions in the Michelin Guide. These restaurants provide superb food, outstanding service, and a wonderful experience. They are:

Bhoga: A restaurant that follows the principle of 'use everything and waste nothing.' Bhoga produces recipes based on Nordic flavor and fresh vegetables from small, neighboring farms. The menu varies every day based on what is available.

Koka: A restaurant that aspires to be fun and charming rather than stuffy and uptight. Koka delivers Swedish and contemporary cuisine, fully meat-free, with 90 percent organic goods. The recipes, such as beets with goat cheese and walnuts, are basic yet elegant.

Project: A comfortable and pleasant restaurant that originated as a café. The project is led by a husband-and-wife pair that seeks to build a second home with well-prepared European meals at moderate pricing. The menu comprises delicacies such as lamb with artichoke and mint or fish with cauliflower and lemon.

28+: A traditional restaurant with white tablecloths and candlelight. 28+ has held a Michelin star for almost 30 years (!) and is equally known for its well-stocked wine cellar. The menu is a combination of French and Swedish cuisine, such as foie gras with apple or venison with lingonberries.

SK Mat & Människor: An intimate restaurant with cuisine based on Swedish gastronomic history. Here, you can be guaranteed to have all your gourmet queries answered — the chefs bring the meals, and there are no boundaries between you and the kitchen. The menu offers smoked salmon with horseradish cream or duck breast with black currant sauce.

Affordable bistros

If you are searching for exceptional and economical eating, check out the Bib Gourmand restaurants in Gothenburg. Bib Gourmand is a component of the Michelin Guide that honors places notable for their excellent value for money. Gothenburg has two Bib Gourmand restaurants:

Familjen: A restaurant that was chosen as the most loveable restaurant of the year in 2018. Familjen delivers modern West Swedish food with large quantities and cheerful service. The menu includes hog belly with cabbage or fish with mussel soup.

Somm: A restaurant and wine bar where the pairing of cuisine and drink is crucial. Somm provides set dinners centered on Nordic cuisine with worldwide influences. The meals are complemented by carefully picked wines from across the globe.

Classic restaurants

If you are craving Swedish comfort food, Gothenburg offers several eateries that provide classic 'husmanskost' like meatballs and herring. These are some of the iconic restaurants in Gothenburg:

Berzelius Bar & Matsal: A Swedish brasserie famed for its meatballs. The lunch menu comprises substantial traditional foods, but the à la carte menu also contains current elements such as Swedish tapas. The restaurant features a comfortable and stylish atmosphere with an Art-Deco style.

Kåges Hörna: A restaurant in Stora Saluhallen, Gothenburg's biggest indoor market hall. The lunch menu focuses on cheap, traditional meals and always offers a daily 'husman' dish. You may also get meals at Kågebaren, just around the corner.

Kometen: Another legendary Gothenburg restaurant, Kometen has attracted the city's creative crowd since 1934. The menu comprises delicacies such as fried herring with mashed potatoes, beef Rydberg or apple pie with vanilla sauce.

This chapter has given you a taste of Gothenburg's broad and lively culinary scene, where you can get anything from fresh seafood to Michelin-starred cuisine. Gothenburg is a city that cherishes its culinary culture, emphasizing sustainability, quality, and inventiveness. Whether searching for a nice cafe, a fine dining restaurant, or a street food market, you will find something to fit your palette and budget in Gothenburg.

CHAPTER 2

Attractions and Sightseeing

Gothenburg is a city that has a lot to offer, from its historical and cultural sites to its natural and urban attractions to its fun and leisure possibilities. You may discover something that will fit your taste, whether interested in art, architecture, science, nature, or adventure. You may explore the city's history, present, and future in museums, monuments, and neighborhoods. You may experience the city's beauty, variety, and creativity in its parks, gardens, and galleries. You may have fun at the city's amusement park, festivals, and events. In this chapter, we will guide you through some of the attractions and sightseeing possibilities you may enjoy during your vacation to Gothenburg.

The Feskekörka fish market and the seafood restaurants

Gothenburg is a city that loves fish. The city's position on the west coast of Sweden, between the Kattegat Strait and the North Sea, affords access to some of the freshest and tastiest seafood and shellfish in the world. You may sample the abundance of the sea at the Feskekörka fish market and the seafood restaurants in Gothenburg.

The Feskekörka fish market

The Feskekörka fish market is one of Gothenburg's most distinctive and popular attractions. The term Feskekörka means "fish church" in Swedish, and it alludes to the form of the tower, which resembles a Gothic church. The building was designed by Victor von Gegerfelt and erected in 1874. It is situated on the Rosenlund Canal, near the City Museum and the Kronhuset.

The Feskekörka fish market is heaven for seafood lovers. You may find a variety of fish and shellfish, such as salmon, cod, herring, mackerel, shrimp, lobster, crab, oyster, mussels, and scallops. You may also discover smoked, cured, pickled, or marinated fish items, such as gravlax, kippers, rollmops, or surströmming. You may purchase fresh or cooked fish from the booths and sellers within the market or order from the restaurants and cafés on the top level. You may also enjoy some live music or art shows in the market.

The Feskekörka fish market is open from Monday through Saturday, from 10:00 to 18:00. It is closed on Sundays and public holidays. You may reach the market via tram, bus, bike, or foot from the city center. You may also take a boat cruise to the market from Lilla Bommen or Stenpiren.

The seafood eateries

Gothenburg has a rich and diversified culinary culture, with influences from both the sea and the land. You may discover restaurants, cafés, bars, and pubs that provide wonderful food and drink from many cuisines and cultures. However, if you want to feel the authentic flavor of Gothenburg, you should visit some of the seafood restaurants in the city.

You can find some of the top seafood restaurants in Gothenburg near the Feskekörka fish market, such as:

Sjömagasinet: a restaurant that is located in a former storehouse from 1775. It has a Michelin star and a Bib Gourmand award. It delivers traditional Swedish meals with a contemporary touch, utilizing fresh and local ingredients. Some delicacies include smoked eel with horseradish cream, grilled turbot with browned butter sauce, and baked Alaska with cloudberries.

Fiskekrogen: a restaurant launched in 1989 by Leif Mannerström, one of Sweden's most recognized chefs. It has a Bib Gourmand award and a White Guide recommendation. It delivers classic and innovative seafood dishes with an international flair. Some favorites include lobster soup with saffron aioli, halibut with truffle mashed potatoes, and crème brûlée with sea buckthorn sorbet.

Feskekôrka: a restaurant that is situated within the Feskekörka fish market. It features a relaxed and pleasant environment. It delivers simple and fresh fish meals with a Nordic twist. Some possibilities are fish soup with aioli and croutons, fried herring with mashed potatoes and lingonberries, and grilled salmon with dill sauce and boiled potatoes.

You can find some of the top seafood restaurants in Gothenburg in other sections of the city, such as:

Gabriel is a restaurant on the second level of the Stora Saluhallen, a historic food hall in the city center. It has a White Guide recommendation and a Certificate of Excellence from TripAdvisor. It delivers unique and beautiful fish dishes with a Mediterranean flavor. Some possibilities include oysters with champagne vinaigrette, scallops with cauliflower puree and truffle oil, and fish with tomato and basil sauce.

Heaven 23: a restaurant on the 23rd story of the Gothia Towers, a hotel and conference center near the Liseberg Amusement Park. It boasts a wonderful view of the city and the water. It delivers innovative and elegant fish dishes with a Scandinavian flair. Some highlights are lobster salad with avocado and mango, monkfish with saffron risotto and asparagus, and king crab with garlic butter and fries.

Sjöbaren: a restaurant in the Haga district, a pleasant and intimate place with wooden buildings and cobblestone lanes. It offers a rustic and intimate vibe. It delivers traditional and substantial fish meals with a Swedish flair. Some possibilities are fish stew with rouille and cheese, smoked salmon with potato salad and mustard sauce, and fried cod with remoulade and boiled potatoes.

Gothenburg is a city that loves fish. The city's position on the west coast of Sweden, between the Kattegat Strait and the North Sea, affords it access to some of the freshest and tastiest seafood and shellfish in the world. You may sample the abundance of the sea at the Feskekörka fish market and the seafood restaurants in Gothenburg.

The Universeum scientific center and the tropical rainforest
If you are searching for a fun and instructive trip to Gothenburg, you should take advantage of the Universeum scientific center, the biggest in Scandinavia. This fascinating site provides a range of activities and displays that will stimulate your curiosity and creativity and bring you closer to nature and science.

One of the most spectacular elements of the Universeum is the tropical rainforest, a seven-story high indoor habitat that recreates the richness and temperature of the Amazon. Here you may experience more than 200 kinds of creatures and vegetation, such as monkeys, sloths, toucans, piranhas, orchids, and cocoa trees. You may also explore several levels of the rainforest, from the canopy to the forest floor, and learn about the problems and potential of this crucial habitat.

The Universeum also boasts a stunning ocean zone where you can witness more than 100 kinds of marine life, such as sharks, rays, turtles, corals, and clownfish. You may marvel at the 1.4 million liter Ocean Tank, where you can see feeding displays and diving shows with actual divers. You may also visit the Swedish West Coast Aquarium, where you can witness the natural fish and creatures of the Gothenburg archipelago. And if you are feeling bold, you may touch some of the species in the Ray Tank, such as starfish, sea urchins, and crabs.

But that's not all. The Universeum also features other intriguing parts that appeal to diverse interests and ages. For example:

Kalejdo: A area where you may examine themes such as criminal investigation, laser, space, etc. You can also see 3D movies at the Wisdom Gothenburg Dome cinema, which provides spectacular experiences of 8K quality.

Explora: A part where you may explore chemistry, physics, biology, and technology. You may also learn about the human body and mind at the Humans exhibition, which offers interactive exhibits and activities.

Water's Way: A part where you may explore Sweden's freshwater and brackish water habitats. You may also observe reptiles and voles that dwell near water.

Deadly Beauties: A part where you may view some of the most poisonous and deadly reptiles in the world, such as cobras, vipers, rattlesnakes, crocodiles, and lizards.

The Universeum is where you may have fun while learning new things. You may also attend guided tours, seminars, presentations, and events arranged by the staff and professionals. The Universeum is open every day of the year, from 10 am to 6 pm (except on Christmas Eve). The entry cost is 245 SEK for adults and 195 SEK for youngsters (4-16 years old). You may also purchase a package that includes a dome show for 310 SEK for adults and 260 SEK for youngsters. You may purchase your tickets online or at the entrance.

The Universeum is situated on Korsvägen, adjacent to Liseberg Amusement Park and the Swedish Exhibition & Congress Centre. You may easily access there by public transport (tram or bus), by vehicle (parking provided), or by bike (bike racks available). You may also find a restaurant and a café within the Universeum, where you can eat sustainable and tasty cuisine.

The Universeum is a must-see attraction for anybody who loves nature and science. It is a destination where you may experience the marvels of the globe in one day.

Liseberg amusement park and the roller coasters

Liseberg is one of the most popular attractions in Gothenburg and Scandinavia, drawing around three million tourists yearly. The amusement park started in 1923 as part of the Gothenburg Exhibition and has since developed to become a world-class destination for pleasure and enjoyment. Liseberg has everything for everyone, from exhilarating rides and games to concerts and events, from restaurants and cafés to gardens and sculptures. You will find it at Liseberg, whether you are seeking excitement, romance, or family pleasure.

One of the greatest attractions in Liseberg is the roller coasters. The park offers six roller coasters that appeal to varying degrees of adrenaline and adventure. Here are some of the highlights of the roller coasters in Liseberg:

Balder: Balder is a wooden roller coaster launched in 2003 and has been selected twice as the greatest wooden roller coaster in the world. Balder boasts a 70-degree drop, a 90 km/h peak speed, and a track length of 1,070 meters. Balder is a smooth and rapid ride that will make you feel like you are soaring through the skies.

Helix: Helix is a steel roller coaster premiered in 2014 and hailed for its design and creativity. Helix contains seven inversions, two launches, and a 100 km/h peak speed. Helix is a twisted and challenging route that will take you on a tour through the hills and woods of Liseberg.

Valkyria: Valkyria is a steel dive coaster that premiered in 2018 and has been described as Europe's longest and tallest dive coaster. Valkyria boasts a 50-meter vertical drop, a 105 km/h peak speed, and a track length of 750 meters. Valkyria is a magnificent and intense trip that makes you feel like diving into the abyss.

Loke: Loke is a gigantic pendulum ride that premiered in 2017 and has been hailed as the most extreme attraction at Liseberg. Loke swings riders up to 42 meters high at an angle of 120 degrees, reaching a speed of 100 km/h. Loke is an exciting and dangerous journey that will make you feel like you are confronting the wrath of the Norse god of mischief.

AtmosFear: AtmosFear is a free-fall tower that debuted in 2011 and has been recognized as the highest free-fall tower in Europe. AtmosFear lowers riders from a height of 116 meters at a speed of 110 km/h, generating a sense of weightlessness. AtmosFear is a spine-chilling and nerve-wracking journey that will make you feel like you are falling from the sky.

Luna: Luna is a boomerang roller coaster that premiered in 2023 and has been touted as the new headline attraction at Liseberg. Luna pushes riders forward and backward over loops, twists, and bends, reaching a speed of 85 km/h. Luna is a lively and dynamic ride that will make you feel like you are enjoying two rides in one.

Liseberg is a location where you may have a lot of fun and excitement with your friends, family, or partner. You may enjoy the roller coasters that provide varying degrees of excitement and adventure and other rides, games, shows, and attractions. Liseberg is a location where you may have amazing moments and enjoy the thrill of entertainment. This chapter has provided you with valuable information and advice on arranging your vacation to Liseberg and making the most of your stay.

The Skansen Kronan Fortress and the panoramic views

The Skansen Kronan Fortress and the panoramic views of Gothenburg are a city with a rich and intriguing history, and one of the greatest sites to explore is the Skansen Kronan Castle. This remarkable edifice lies on a hilltop in the Haga neighborhood, affording a spectacular view of the city and its surroundings. Here are some reasons to visit the Skansen Kronan fortress and enjoy the panoramic views.

The history of the fortification

The Skansen Kronan fortification was erected in the late 17th century as part of the defensive system of Gothenburg. It was planned by Erik Dahlberg, a military engineer, and architect who also worked on the Skansen Lejonet stronghold on the other side of the city. The castle was finished in 1700; it contained 23 guns and a garrison of 300 troops. It was ready for combat, yet adversaries never assaulted it.

The stronghold had numerous uses throughout the ages, such as a jail, an emergency residency, a military museum, and a private house. Today, it is a cultural heritage site and a location for events such as weddings, parties, and conferences.

The architecture of the fortification

The Skansen Kronan fortress is a unique example of Swedish baroque architecture, with a circular design, a conical roof, and four corner towers. It is composed of red bricks and granite stones, contrasting with the green surrounding. The stronghold has two levels and a basement, with a total size of 800 square meters. The interior boasts a distinctive hall with a dome roof adorned with paintings and sculptures.

A moat encircles the stronghold and a wall constructed in the 18th century. There is also a garden with flowers and trees, where you may rest and enjoy the outdoors.

The view from the castle

The Skansen Kronan fortification gives a spectacular perspective of Gothenburg and its countryside. You can view the ancient town, the port, the river Göta älv, the bridges, the islands, and the hills. You may also observe some of the city's monuments, such as the Feskekörka fish market, the Liseberg amusement park, the Ullevi stadium, and the Gothia Towers hotel.

The vista is particularly spectacular around sunset when the sky transforms into numerous colors of orange, pink, and purple. You may also appreciate the city lights at night, creating a beautiful ambiance.

How to get there

The Skansen Kronan fortress is situated atop Risåsberget hill in the Haga district, approximately 2 kilometers from the city center. You may reach there by public transport, by bike or by foot.

By public transport: You may take bus number 60 from Brunnsparken or Järntorget to Haga Kyrkoplan stop. You may walk up to the castle via Skansgatan Street or take steps from Kaponjärgatan Street.

By bike: You may hire a bike from one of the numerous stations in Gothenburg and go to the Haga district. There are bike racks at Haga Kyrkoplan stop where you may store your bike.

By foot: You may stroll to the Haga district from the city center via Kungsgatan Street or Vasagatan Street. Then you may take Skansgatan Street or Kaponjärgatan Street up to the fortification.

When to go

The Skansen Kronan fortress is open all year round. However, it has variable opening hours depending on the season. Please verify them on their website or phone them before you go.

Spring (March-May): The stronghold is open on weekends from 12:00 to 16:00. The garden is in blossom and the weather is warm.

Summer (June-August): The stronghold is open every day from 11:00 to 18:00. The patio is available for food and beverages. The view is clear and bright.

Autumn (September-November): The stronghold is open on weekends from 12:00 to 16:00. The garden is changing hues, and the weather is chilly.

Winter (December-February): The stronghold is open on weekends from 12:00 to 16:00. The roof is covered with snow, and the weather is frigid.

This sub chapter has given you a peek at the Skansen Kronan fortress and the panoramic views in Gothenburg, where you may explore this remarkable tower's history, architecture, and beauty. Skansen Kronan is a cultural heritage site, a location for events, and a place to rest and appreciate the environment and the cityscape. Whether interested in history, art, or photography, you can find something to suit your interests at Skansen Kronan. Take the chance to visit the Skansen Kronan fortress, enjoy the panoramic views in Gothenburg, and understand why this city is a historical and cultural jewel.

The Haga district and the huge cinnamon buns

Gothenburg is a city that has a lot of charm and character, and one of the greatest locations to enjoy is the Haga neighborhood. The Haga neighborhood is one of the oldest and most scenic sections of Gothenburg, with wooden buildings, cobblestone lanes, and quiet cafés. The Haga region is particularly famed for its huge cinnamon buns, a delightful and decadent delicacy you should not miss.

The history of the Haga district

The Haga district was developed in the 17th century as one of the original suburbs of Gothenburg. It was initially occupied by laborers, artisans, and sailors, who erected their houses and stores along the main street, Haga Nagata. The region was named after Queen Hedvig Eleonora, who owned the land where it was situated.

The Haga neighborhood was a dynamic and varied region with various cultures and faiths. It was also a location of social movements and changes, such as the temperance, labor, and women's movements. The area was also devastated by wars, fires, diseases, and poverty, which molded its history and character.

In the 19th century, the Haga quarter grew congested and decrepit as more people flocked to the city. The region was designated a slum, and many structures were removed or neglected. In the 20th century, the Haga neighborhood faced the prospect of urban renewal, which sought to replace its historic buildings with modern flats and offices. However, owing to the efforts of local citizens and activists, the Haga quarter was conserved and restored as a cultural heritage site.

The attractions of the Haga district

Today, the Haga neighborhood is one of the most popular and picturesque places in Gothenburg. You may discover numerous activities to see and do in this attractive area, such as:

The Haga Nygata: the major street of the Haga neighborhood, where you may wander along the cobblestone pavement and appreciate the wooden homes that date back to the 18th and 19th centuries. You may also discover numerous stores, cafés, restaurants, and galleries providing various products and services, from antiques and handicrafts to books and apparel.

The Skansen Kronan is a stronghold erected in 1687 on a hill overlooking Gothenburg. It was created by Erik Dahlbergh, a notable Swedish architect and engineer. It was meant to defend the city against Danish assaults but never saw any action. Today, it is a museum and a location for events.

The Hagabadet is a bathhouse established in 1876 by Peter Wieselgren, a clergyman and social reformer. It was one of the earliest public baths in Sweden, and it included services such as swimming pools, saunas, showers, massage rooms, and gymnastics halls. It also featured cultural events such as concerts, talks, and exhibits. Today, it is a spa and wellness facility that provides treatments and relaxation.

The Café Husaren is a café that is situated on Haga Nygata 28. It is famed for its gigantic cinnamon buns, Hagabullar or Queen's cakes. These buns are roughly 30 cm in diameter and weigh about 1 kilogram. They are prepared using flour, butter, sugar, cinnamon, cardamom, yeast, milk, and eggs. They are baked on huge pans and then sliced into pieces. They are served with butter, cheese, jam, or whipped cream. They are a delightful and luxurious delicacy that you should not miss.

The Haga neighborhood is one of the oldest and most scenic sections of Gothenburg, with wooden buildings, cobblestone lanes, and quiet cafés. The Haga region is particularly famed for its huge cinnamon buns, a delightful and decadent delicacy you should not miss.

The Gothenburg Museum of Art and the Nordic collections

If you are a fan of art, you should take advantage of the Gothenburg Museum of Art, one of Scandinavia's most prominent and extensive art museums. This museum, situated in Götaplatsen square, has a collection of about 70 000 pieces, ranging from the 15th century to now, largely from Europe and the USA. However, the museum's major appeal is its unique and excellent collection of Nordic art from about the turn of the century 1900, which is regarded as one of the world's greatest.

The Nordic collection is shown in numerous rooms, but the most renowned and popular one is the Fürstenberg Gallery, which fills the whole top floor of the museum. Pontus and Göthilda Fürstenberg presented this gallery to the museum, a rich couple who were passionate art collectors and patrons in Gothenburg towards the end of the 19th century. They purchased some of the most significant and influential works by Nordic artists of their period, such as Anders Zorn, Carl Larsson, Bruno Liljefors, Edvard Munch, Vilhelm Hammershøi, Helene Schjerfbeck, and Akseli Gallen-Kallela.

The Fürstenberg Gallery provides a unique glimpse into the lively and diversified art environment in the Nordic nations during the 1880s and 1890s when artists experimented with new styles, methods, and topics. You may enjoy paintings that show scenes from ordinary life, nature, history, mythology, and symbolism. You may also discover photographs that show the personalities and feelings of the artists and their models. You may also enjoy using color, light, and brushwork that create diverse moods and atmospheres.

The Fürstenberg Gallery is not only a feast for the eyes but also a historical and cultural record that depicts the social changes and struggles that took place in the Nordic area around the turn of the century 1900. You may learn about the role of women in art and society, the effect of industrialization and urbanization, the emergence of nationalism and regionalism, and the influence of other creative movements like Impressionism and Expressionism. The Gothenburg Museum of Work also contains additional areas that present more Nordic work from other eras and genres. For example:

- In the Swedish Modernism area, you may examine works by artists who Henri Matisse and other French modernists, such as Isaac Grünewald, Sigrid Hjertén, Nils Dardel, and Einar Jolin inspired.

- In the Gothenburg Colourists area, you may examine works by painters prioritizing color above form, such as Åke Göransson, Ivan Ivarson, Ragnar Sandberg, and Inge Schiöler.

- The Arosenius Room area, where you can view works by Ivar Arosenius, a unique and original artist who produced humorous and moving images with his watercolors and drawings.

- The Gothenburg Museum of Art is a must-see destination for anybody who enjoys art and wants to understand more about the Nordic cultural legacy. The museum is open every day except Mondays, from 11 am to 5 pm (until 8 pm on Wednesdays). The entry charge is 60 SEK for adults (free for children under 25). You may also purchase a combo ticket that includes entrance to other museums in Gothenburg for 100 SEK. You may purchase your tickets online or at the entrance.

The Gothenburg Museum of Art is situated in Götaplatsen Plaza, near the City Theatre and the Concert Hall. You may easily access there by public transport (tram or bus), by vehicle (parking provided), or by bike (bike racks available).

You may also locate a café within the museum, where you can bite or a drink.

The Gothenburg Museum of Art is a site where you may witness some of the best examples of Nordic art from about the turn of the century 1900. It is a location where you may appreciate beauty, study history, and feel inspired.

CHAPTER 3: Nature and Outdoors

Gothenburg is a city surrounded by nature and provides many options for outdoor activities and sports. You may enjoy the fresh air and wonderful views in parks such as Slottsskogen, Botanical Garden, Killers Park, or stroll along the Göta Canal or the Älvsborg Bridge. You may also get on a bike and explore the city on two wheels or join a guided bike trip with Pickup. If you feel brave, you may try kayaking, sailing, fishing, or surfing on the waterways near Gothenburg. You may also explore several of the islands in the southern archipelago by ferry or boat excursion. You may relax on sandy beaches, swim in clean water, trek on gorgeous paths, or enjoy local cuisine and culture. This chapter will guide you through parks, zoos, and hiking trails you should visit for environment enthusiasts.

The Slottsskogen Park and the zoo

Gothenburg is a city surrounded by nature and provides many options for outdoor activities and sports. One of the greatest spots to enjoy the fresh air and breathtaking views is Slottsskogen park and the zoo. The Slottsskogen Park and the Zoo are one of Gothenburg's biggest and most popular parks. It has an area of 137 hectares and is situated southwest of the city. It was created in 1874 by August Kobb, a rich businessman and philanthropist. He gave the property to the city and commissioned landscape architect Peter Ekman to build the park. The park provides a range of attractions and activities, such as:

The zoo: a free zoo that houses creatures such as moose, deer, seals, penguins, owls, and goats. You may also view several rare and endangered animals, such as the Swedish woodland reindeer, the Gotland pony, and the European bison. The zoo is open all year round from 10:00 to 16:00 (or 17:00 in summer). You may reach the zoo via tram, bus, bike, or foot from the city center.

The children's zoo: a zoo that is specifically built for children, where they may engage with animals such as rabbits, guinea pigs, chickens, ducks, and pigs. They may also play in the playgrounds, ride on the carousel, or take a train trip around the park. The children's zoo is open from April to October from 10:00 to 16:00 (or 17:00 in summer). You may reach the children's zoo via tram, bus, bike, or foot from the city center.

The natural history museum: a museum that displays exhibits and artifacts connected to nature and animals. You may observe fossils, bones, stuffed animals, insects, shells, minerals, and plants. You may also learn about themes like evolution, ecology, climate change, and biodiversity. The museum is open from Tuesday through Sunday from 11:00 to 17:00 (or 18:00 in summer). You may reach the museum via tram, bus, bike, or foot from the city center.

The observatory: an observatory that was established in 1923 by Carl Charlier, a notable Swedish astronomer. It features a dome-shaped roof that can be opened to show a telescope. You may visit the observatory during special events or organize a private appointment to study the stars and planets. The observatory is situated on a hill near the

Skansen Kronan castle. You may reach the observatory via tram, bus, bike, or foot from the city center.

The Azalea Valley: a valley that is filled with hundreds of azaleas, rhododendrons, magnolias, and other blooming plants. It is one of the most attractive sites in the park, particularly during spring and summer when the flowers are in full bloom. You may also discover several ponds, streams, bridges, and sculptures throughout the valley. The valley is situated near the main entrance of the park on Linnéplatsen. You may access the valley via tram, bus, bike, or foot from the city center.

The Slottsskogen Park and the Zoo are one of Gothenburg's biggest and most popular parks. It has an area of 137 hectares and is situated southwest of the city. It was created in 1874 by August Kobb, a rich businessman and philanthropist. He gave the property to the city and commissioned landscape architect Peter Ekman to build the park. The park provides a range of attractions and activities, such as:

The zoo: a free zoo that houses creatures such as moose, deer, seals, penguins, owls, and goats. You may also view several rare and endangered animals, such as the Swedish woodland reindeer, the Gotland pony, and the European bison. The zoo is open all year round from 10:00 to 16:00 (or 17:00 in summer). You may reach the zoo via tram, bus, bike, or foot from the city center.

The children's zoo: a zoo that is specifically built for children, where they may engage with animals such as rabbits, guinea pigs, chickens, ducks, and pigs. They may also play in the playgrounds, ride on the carousel, or take a train trip around the park. The children's zoo is open from April to October from 10:00 to 16:00 (or 17:00 in summer). You may reach the children's zoo via tram, bus, bike, or foot from the city center.

The natural history museum: a museum that displays exhibits and artifacts connected to nature and animals. You may observe fossils, bones, stuffed animals, insects, shells, minerals, and plants. You may also learn about themes like evolution, ecology, climate change, and biodiversity. The museum is open from Tuesday through Sunday from 11:00

to 17:00 (or 18:00 in summer). You may reach the museum via tram, bus, bike, or foot from the city center.

The observatory: an observatory that was established in 1923 by Carl Charlier, a notable Swedish astronomer. It features a dome-shaped roof that can be opened to show a telescope. You may visit the observatory during special events or organize a private appointment to study the stars and planets. The observatory is situated on a hill near the Skansen Kronan castle. You may reach the observatory via tram, bus, bike, or foot from the city center.

The Azalea Valley: a valley that is filled with hundreds of azaleas, rhododendrons, magnolias, and other blooming plants. It is one of the most attractive sites in the park, particularly during spring and summer when the flowers are in full bloom. You may also discover several ponds, streams, bridges, and sculptures throughout the valley. The valley is situated near the main entrance of the park on Linnéplatsen. You may access the valley via tram, bus, bike, or foot from the city center.

The Slottsskogen Park and the zoo is an excellent spot to explore nature and outdoors in Gothenburg. You may observe and learn about various animals and plants, play and relax in the playgrounds and picnic spaces, or appreciate the vistas and sculptures in the park. You may also join some of the events and activities in the park throughout the year, such as concerts, festivals, fairs, and sports. The Slottsskogen Park and the zoo is a destinations that will make you feel pleased and rejuvenated.

The Botanical Garden and the greenhouses

Suppose you are seeking a quiet and refreshing retreat from the city. In that case, you should visit the Botanical Garden and the greenhouses, one of the most attractive and interesting attractions in Gothenburg. This location, situated in the south of the city, encompasses an area of 175 hectares, of which 40 are developed as a garden and 135 are a natural reserve. Here you may enjoy a variety of plants, flowers, trees, and landscapes, as well as learn about botany, ecology, and conservation.

The Botanical Garden was established in 1923 and opened publicly in 1928. It features a collection of about 16 000 types of plants, divided into various divisions according to their origin, habitat, or usage. Some of the attractions of the garden are:

1. The Rock Garden, where you may observe alpine plants from other continents, such as gentians, primulas, saxifrages, and edelweiss.

2. The Rhododendron Valley, where you may view more than 500 types of rhododendrons and azaleas, as well as magnolias, camellias, and hydrangeas.

3. The Herb Garden, where you may learn about herbs' medicinal, culinary, and fragrant characteristics, such as lavender, rosemary, mint, and sage.

4. The Japanese Glade, where you may enjoy a quiet and harmonious ambiance inspired by Japanese gardens, with a pond, a bridge, a pavilion, and flora such as bamboo, cherry trees, and peonies.

5. The Kitchen Garden is where you can view vegetables, fruits, berries, and flowers cultivated organically and utilized in the garden's café.

The greenhouses are situated near the Botanical Garden and were erected in 1971. They have a total space of 1000 square meters and host more than 4000 types of plants from tropical and subtropical climates. Some of the highlights of the greenhouses are:

- The Palm House, where you may observe palms, cycads, bananas, figs, and other plants that flourish in warm and humid areas.

- The Orchid House, where you may observe more than 1500 types of orchids from all over the globe, as well as bromeliads, ferns, and carnivorous plants.

- The Succulent House, where you may discover more than 1000 kinds of succulents from dry locations, such as cactus, aloes, agaves, and euphorbias.

- The Victoria House, where you may marvel at the huge water lily Victoria amazonica, has leaves up to 3 meters in diameter and blossoms up to 40 centimeters wide.

The Botanical Garden and the greenhouses are open every day of the year. The garden is open from dawn to sunset (or until 9 pm in summer), and the entrance is free. The greenhouses are open from 10 am to 5 pm (or until 8 pm on Wednesdays), and entry is 20 SEK for adults (free for children under 18). You may also attend guided tours or seminars offered by the staff or volunteers. You may also visit the garden's store and café, where you can purchase plants, seeds, books, souvenirs, or have a snack or a drink.

The Botanical Garden and the greenhouses are situated in Änggården, near Slottsskogen Park. You may easily reach them by public transport (tram or bus), by vehicle (parking provided), or by bike (bike racks available). You may also walk from the city center (approximately 3 kilometers) or Linnéplatsen (about 1 kilometer).

The Botanical Garden and the greenhouses are amazing places to enjoy nature's beauty, variety, and amazement. It is a location where you may rest, study, and have fun.

The Southern Archipelago and the car-free islands

Gothenburg is a busy metropolis and a gateway to a beautiful and quiet archipelago. The Southern Archipelago comprises roughly 20 islands readily accessible by boat from Saltholmen or Stenpiren. The islands are car-free, meaning you can enjoy the archipelago's beauty, peace, and attractiveness without any noise or pollution. The islands provide a range of activities and attractions, from swimming and kayaking to hiking and bicycling, fishing and sailing to art and culture. Whether searching for a day vacation or a longer stay, you will find something to fit your taste and interest in the Southern Archipelago. Here are some of the highlights of the Southern Archipelago and the car-free islands:

Styrsö: Styrsö is the biggest and most inhabited island in the Southern Archipelago, with roughly 1,400 residents. Styrsö contains four villages: Styrsö Tången, Styrsö Bratten, Styrsö Skäret, and Styrsö Sandvik. Each community has its character and history from the 17th century. Styrsö is a popular site for swimming, sunbathing, and strolling. You may visit the Styrsö Church, which was completed in 1752 and has a lovely wooden interior. You may also enjoy the views from the Styrsö Skäret observation tower erected in 1899 as a fire watchtower. You may also explore the island by bike or foot, following the established routes through woods, meadows, and cliffs.

Donsö: Donsö is a nearby island to Styrsö, linked by a bridge. Donsö has roughly 1,400 residents and is noted for its fishing and shipping business. Donsö has a port where you can observe the fishing boats and the trade ships that cruise throughout the globe. You may also visit the Donsö Museum, which highlights the history and culture of the island and its inhabitants. You may also appreciate the beauty and fauna of Donsö, such as the seals that reside on the rocks along the coast. You may also swim or kayak in the pristine sea or walk or cycle on the island's pathways.

Vrångö: Vrångö is the southernmost island in the Southern Archipelago, with roughly 380 residents. Vrångö is a natural reserve that features some of the archipelago's most pristine and diversified landscapes. You may discover sandy beaches, rocky shorelines, pine woods, heather fields, and wetlands on Vrångö. You may also observe numerous birds and flora that are uncommon or endangered in other regions of Sweden. You may enjoy swimming, fishing, sailing, or birding on Vrångö. You may also trek or cycle on the paths that bring you to other portions of the island, such as the lighthouse, the church, or the ancient fishing town.

Brännö: Brännö is another island in the Southern Archipelago, with roughly 900 residents. Brännö is famed for its traditional dances that take place every Thursday evening throughout the summer in Brännö Husvik. You may join the residents and guests who dance to live music on a wooden dance floor near the sea. You may also enjoy swimming or sunbathing at one of Brännö's beaches, such as Sjöstugans Badplats or Ramsdal. You may also explore Brännö by foot or bike, following the routes linking the island's various portions, such as the church, the school, or the harbor.

In conclusion, the Southern Archipelago and the car-free islands are terrific opportunities to escape the city's hustle and bustle and enjoy nature's beauty and tranquillity. You may visit the islands by boat and explore them on foot or by bike. On the islands, you may swim, fish, sail, kayak, walk, cycle, or birdwatch. You may also enjoy the culture and history of the islands, such as the traditional dances, the fishing villages, the cathedrals, and the museums. The Southern Archipelago and the car-free islands are where you may rest, refuel, and reconnect with yourself and your loved ones. This chapter has provided valuable information and advice on arranging your vacation to the Southern Archipelago and the car-free islands and making the most of your stay.

The Delsjön Lake and the hiking pathways

Gothenburg has many green places to enjoy nature and outdoor activities. One of the greatest locations to accomplish so is the Delsjön region, a natural reserve that consists of two linked lakes, Stora Delsjön and Lilla Delsjön, and a network of hiking routes. Here are some reasons you should visit Delsjön Lake and the hiking routes.

The splendor of the lake

The Delsjön Lake is a lovely sight with pure water, forested shoreline, and rocky islets. You may observe the lake from several angles, such as a beach, a bridge, a boat, or a vantage point. The lake also has numerous fauna, including birds, fish, frogs, and beavers.

The lake is a popular site for swimming, fishing, kayaking, and canoeing. You may hire a boat or a kayak from one of the rental stations surrounding the lake or bring your equipment. You may also find various areas to enjoy a picnic or a BBQ beside the lake.

The diversity of the hiking pathways

The Delsjön region contains various hiking paths that fit varying degrees of ability and interest. You may pick from short or long loops, simple or tough courses, woodland, or moorland walks. You may also mix several paths to make your itinerary.

Some of the more popular hiking paths in the Delsjön region are:

Stora Delsjön – Lilla Delsjön Loop: A moderate walk circuits both lakes, traveling through woodland, meadow, and wetland habitats. The route is roughly 10 kilometers long and takes around 3 hours.

Stora Delsjön Loop: An simple track that encircles Stora Delsjön, following primarily gravel roads. The route is roughly 8 kilometers long and takes around 2 hours.

Bohusleden Stage 3: Skatås - Kåsjön: A moderate track part of the Bohusleden, a long-distance hiking trail extending through southwest Sweden. The route travels through the natural reserve Knipeflågsbergen, which borders the Delsjön region, and terminates at Kåsjön Lake. The route is roughly 10 kilometers long and takes around 3 hours.

Lilla Delsjön Loop: An simple walk that encircles just Lilla Delsjön, using primarily woodland pathways. The route is roughly 5 kilometers long and takes around 1 hour.

How to get there

The Delsjön region is situated east of Gothenburg, approximately 5 kilometers from the city center. You may reach there via public transport, by bike or by automobile.

By public transport: You may take tram number 5 from Korsvägen or Järntorget to Skatås station. From there, you may stroll to the lake or follow the instructions to one of the hiking routes.

By bike: You may hire a bike at one of the numerous stations in Gothenburg and pedal to the Skatås stop. There are bike racks where you may store your bike.

By vehicle: You may drive to Skatås station and park in one of the parking lots nearby.

When to go

The Delsjön region is accessible all year round. However, it has varied attractions depending on the season. You may check the weather forecast and the operating hours of the rental stations before you travel.

Spring (March-May): A fantastic season to appreciate the flowering flowers, the green trees, and the fresh air. The weather might be unpredictable, so pack clothes and a raincoat.

Summer (June-August): The prime season for tourists, with pleasant weather, bright days, and various activities. The lake is inviting for swimming, boating, and fishing. Book your rental equipment in advance.

Autumn (September-November): A beautiful season to appreciate the changing hues of the leaves, the comfortable environment, and the animals. The weather may be cool and wet, so bring warm clothing and an umbrella.

Winter (December-February): A terrific season to explore the snow-covered countryside, the frozen lake, and the indoor attractions. The weather may be chilly and snowy, so bring a coat and boots.

The Älvsborg fortress and the boat trips

Gothenburg is a city that has a rich and intriguing history stretching back to the ancient periods. The city's position on the mouth of the Göta Älv River, near the Kattegat strait, has made it a strategic and appealing spot for human habitation, commerce, and defense. One of the most significant and magnificent structures that symbolizes this history is the Älvsborg stronghold. This sea fortification secured Sweden's access to the Atlantic Ocean, the surrounding colony of Gothenburg, and its four predecessors. You may see this stronghold and learn about its history and importance by boat excursion from the city center.

The history of the Älvsborg fortress

The Älvsborg stronghold, also known as Elfsborg stronghold or Älvsborgs fästning, is a now-defunct Swedish fortification that was situated near the mouth of the Göta Älv river. The term Älvsborg means "river stronghold" in Swedish, and it alludes to the tower's design, which resembles a Gothic cathedral. The stronghold was moved in the 17th century, and this New Älvsborg stronghold is being maintained today.

The oldest recorded reference to Älvsborg goes back to the 11th century when it was referred to as Geitaborg or Gaetaborg by Adam of Bremen, a German chronicler. He depicted it as a settlement on an island in the Göta Älv River, controlled by a Danish monarch. However, this town was probably around present-day Kungälv, some 20 km north of Gothenburg.

The first effort to erect a fortification on the location of the current Älvsborg was attempted by King Sverker II of Sweden in 1161. He erected a fortress on the southern side of the river, near present-day Lilla Bommen, and called it Götaholm or Gotaholmen. However, this castle was quickly destroyed by the Norwegians in 1164.

The second effort to construct a fortification in the same place was attempted by King Valdemar I of Denmark in 1204. He erected a fortress on the northern side of the river, near present-day Kronhuset, and called it Götaborgh or Gothenburg. However, this castle was likewise short-lived since it was burnt by the Swedes in 1219.

The third effort to erect a fortification in the same place was attempted by King Magnus IV of Sweden in 1323. He erected a fortress on the southern side of the river, near present-day Lilla Bommen, and called it Nya Lödöse or Nyälvsborg. This fortification was more successful than its predecessors since it became a significant commerce hub and a bastion against the Danes. However, this castle was also afflicted by battles, fires, diseases, and floods and was ultimately abandoned in 1473.

The fourth and last effort to erect a stronghold on the location of the present Älvsborg was attempted by King Gustav II Adolf of Sweden in 1621. He awarded the city a royal charter and encouraged Dutch, German, Scottish, and French merchants and artisans to settle there. The city was planned by Dutch engineers, who gave it a grid layout with canals and defenses. The city's name stems from the Old Norse phrase for "fortified town," also used by prior communities on the lower Göta Älv River.

The new stronghold was erected on an island at the mouth of the river near present-day Klippan. It was dubbed Nya Älvsborg or New Älvsborg. It was a vast and spectacular edifice with walls, towers, bastions, moats, and cannons. It was meant to resist assaults from land and sea and to safeguard Sweden's access to the Atlantic Ocean and the adjacent town of Gothenburg.

The new stronghold was vital in Sweden's history, notably during the Thirty Years' War (1618-1648) and the Scanian War (1675-1679). The Danes besieged the citadel multiple times, who demanded hefty ransoms to preserve it from destruction. The stronghold also functioned as a jail for political prisoners, such as King Erik XIV, Queen Kristina, and King Karl XII. The stronghold has received certain royal visitors, including King Gustav III, King Oscar II, and Queen Victoria.

As Sweden's boundaries and ties with its neighbors altered, the castle progressively lost its military significance in the 18th and 19th centuries. The stronghold was deactivated in 1868 and became a museum and a tourist attraction. The stronghold was rebuilt and remodeled multiple times and is presently preserved by the Swedish National Heritage Board.

The boat cruises

One of the greatest ways to explore the Älvsborg fortress and to appreciate the views of Gothenburg and its port is to take a boat excursion from the city center. You may pick from several choices, such as:

The Paddan boats are tiny and open boats that run from April to October. They embark at Kungsportsplatsen, near the City Museum and the Kronhuset. They provide guided tours in Swedish and English, lasting approximately 50 minutes. They carry you around the canals and the river, passing by sights such as the Feskekörka fish market, the Opera House, and the Eriksberg crane. They also carry you to the island of Nya Älvsborg, where you may disembark and visit the fortress for approximately 30 minutes. You may also have some refreshments in the café on the island. The adult ticket is 250 SEK, and it is 125 SEK for children.

The Strömma boats are spacious and luxurious and run from May to September. They leave from Lilla Bommen, near the Göteborg City Museum and the Poseidon monument. They provide guided tours in Swedish and English, lasting approximately 2 hours. They carry you along the river and the port, passing through sights like the Älvsborg Bridge, the Volvo Museum, and the Lindholmen Science Park. They also carry you to the island of Nya Älvsborg, where you may disembark and visit the fortress for around 45 minutes. You may also have some nibbles and beverages in the bar on board. The adult ticket is 295 SEK, and for children is 150 SEK.

The Stromma Archipelago boats include big and luxurious vessels from June to August. They leave from Stenpiren, near the City Museum and the Haga neighborhood. They provide guided tours in Swedish and English, lasting approximately 3 hours. They carry you along the river and the port, passing through sights like the Älvsborg Bridge, the Volvo Museum, and the Lindholmen Science Park. They also transport you to several of the islands in the southern archipelago, such as Styrsö, Brännö, and Vrångö. You may exit and visit the islands for around 30 minutes each. You may also have some nibbles and beverages in the bar on board. The adult fee is 395 SEK, and for children is 200 SEK.

The Älvsborg Castle and the boat cruises are a terrific opportunity to discover the history and beauty of Gothenburg and its environs. You may tour the stronghold and learn about its importance and tales and see the vistas and sculptures on the island. You may also enjoy the boat cruises, explore the city and archipelago from a fresh perspective, and relax and have fun on board. The Älvsborg fortress and the boat trips are a must-do activity during your vacation to Gothenburg.

CHAPTER 4: Shopping and Entertainment

Gothenburg is a city that provides many possibilities for shopping and entertainment, whether you are seeking fashion, design, art, music, or nightlife. You will find everything from worldwide brands to local stores, sophisticated malls, beautiful streets, fashionable clubs, and quiet pubs. Here are some of the top neighborhoods and venues for shopping and entertainment in Gothenburg.

Gothenburg is a city that mixes the cosmopolitan and the historical, the urban and the natural, and the classic and the modern. It is a city that offers something for everyone, regardless of your taste or budget. You may tour the numerous districts and communities of Gothenburg, each with unique character and charm. You may explore the rich cultural and creative legacy of Gothenburg and today's dynamic and inventive scene. You can also enjoy the cheerful and accepting environment of Gothenburg, where you can meet new people and have fun.

This chapter will lead you through some of the greatest neighborhoods and venues to enjoy shopping and entertainment in Gothenburg. We will show you where to discover the city's most popular and prominent boutiques, restaurants, pubs, and cafés. We will also offer advice and suggestions on making the most of your shopping and entertainment experience in Gothenburg. Whether you are searching for a day of shopping, a night of partying, or a combination of both, you can find it in Gothenburg.

The Nordstan retail complex and the fashion shops

If you are seeking a shopping paradise in Gothenburg, you should visit the Nordstan retail mall, Sweden's biggest and most popular shopping destination. This vast complex in the city's center comprises over 200 stores, cafés, and restaurants spread over 320 000 square meters. Here you may discover anything from clothes and accessories to electronics and toys, from local and worldwide brands to independent and specialized boutiques.

One of the major attractions of the Nordstan shopping complex is its excellent assortment of fashion boutiques, where you can discover the newest trends and styles for all tastes and budgets. You may discover some of the most well-known and prominent fashion labels in Nordstan, such as Hugo Boss, Tommy Hilfiger, Ralph Lauren, Tiger of Sweden, Filippa K, Odd Molly, and Rodebjer. You may also find more economical and casual apparel retailers in Nordstan, such as H&M, Zara, Monki, Weekday, and Gina Tricot.

Suppose you are seeking something more distinctive and original. In that case, you may also visit some of the independent and niche fashion boutiques in Nordstan, where you can discover some unusual and quality goods that will make you stand out from the crowd. For example, you should visit:

- Nudie Jeans, a Swedish brand that specializes in organic denim and gives free repairs for life.

- Twist & Tango, a Swedish company that provides sustainable and feminine apparel with a Scandinavian flair.

- Velour, a Gothenburg-based company that mixes traditional tailoring with street-style inspirations.

- Grandpa, a shop that offers antique apparel, accessories, and new things from local and international designers.

The Nordstan retail mall is open every day of the year, from 10 am to 8 pm (except on Sundays, when it shuts at 6 pm).

The entry is free, and you may easily get it by public transport (tram or bus), by vehicle (parking provided), or by bike (bike racks available). You may also have some food and drink at one of the numerous cafés and restaurants in Nordstan, where you can find anything from Swedish delicacies to foreign cuisines.

The Nordstan retail mall is where you can enjoy the finest shopping in Gothenburg. It is a location where you may find everything you need and desire and discover new things. It is a location where you may have fun, relax, and enjoy yourself.

The Avenyn Boulevard and the nightlife venues

Gothenburg is a city that has a lot of beauty and character, and one of the greatest spots to enjoy it is Avenyn Avenue. The Avenyn Boulevard, or Kungsportsavenyen, is the major roadway in Gothenburg. It spans from the bridge Kungsportsbron beside the canal to Götaplatsen and the Museum of Art, the City Theatre, and the Concert Hall. The boulevard is bustling all day till late, with stores, restaurants, cafés, bars, and clubs along both sides of the street. The avenue is also a cultural hotspot, with museums, theatres, galleries, and monuments along the route. Whether searching for shopping, food, entertainment, or art, you will find something for everyone on Avenyn Boulevard.

Shopping on the Avenyn Boulevard

The Avenyn Boulevard is a terrific spot to buy for fashion, design, literature, and more. You may discover worldwide brands and local stores on the street, providing a range of styles and pricing. Some of the popular stores on the boulevard are:

NK: a department store that has been a fixture on the Avenyn since 1915. It provides various items and services, from apparel and accessories to cosmetics and home design. It also features a food hall, a café, and a restaurant.

Designtorget: a shop that offers distinctive and inventive things from Swedish designers. You may get anything from furniture and lighting to jewelry and stationery. It also offers a gallery that promotes fresh and rising talents.

Akademibokhandeln: a bookshop that contains many books in many languages and genres. You may also find magazines, newspapers, games, souvenirs, and stationery. It also features a café where you can have coffee and a pastry.

Grandpa: a shop that offers apparel and accessories with a vintage and retro atmosphere. You may discover both new and second-hand products from Swedish and worldwide companies. It also features a department for home furnishings and leisure items.

Dining on the Avenyn Boulevard

The Avenyn Boulevard is a terrific spot to dine for every occasion and taste. You may discover restaurants that offer cuisines from all over the globe, from Swedish and Scandinavian to Italian and Asian. You may also discover cafés that provide coffee, tea, pastries, sandwiches, and salads. Some of the popular eateries on the boulevard are:
Koka: a restaurant with a Michelin star and a White Guide recommendation. It delivers contemporary Swedish cuisine using fresh and local products.

Some delicacies include smoked eel with horseradish cream, grilled turbot with browned butter sauce, and baked Alaska with cloudberries.

Barabicu: a restaurant that offers meals with inspirations from Latin America, Spain, Portugal, and France. Some of the favorites include lobster soup with saffron aioli, halibut with truffle mashed potatoes, and crème brûlée with sea buckthorn sorbet.

Sassi caffè enoteca: an Italian restaurant and wine bar that provides genuine meals from various areas of Italy.

Some of the possibilities are pizza napoletana , spaghetti carbonara , risotto al funghi , and tiramisu.

Juan Font: a Spanish wine bar that offers tapas , pintxos , paella , sangria , and more. Some of the selections are croquetas de jamón , tortilla española , gambas al ajillo , and churros with chocolate.

Entertainment on the Avenyn Boulevard

The Avenyn Boulevard is a terrific area to have fun at night. You can discover pubs and clubs that appeal to various moods and music inclinations. You may also locate live music venues that showcase concerts and events from local and worldwide performers. Some of the popular pubs and clubs on the boulevard are:

Yaki-Da is a pub and club with three levels with diverse themes and music types. You may discover a rooftop patio, a cocktail bar, a dance floor, and a live stage. You may enjoy music genres such as pop, rock, hip-hop, and house.

Lounge(s): a bar and club that offers a sophisticated and elegant ambiance. You may discover a lounge area, a VIP room, a dance floor, and a balcony. You may appreciate music genres like R&B, soul, funk, and disco.

Sticky Fingers: a pub and club that offers a rock and roll ambiance. You may discover a bar area, a music hall, a dance floor, and a basement. You may appreciate music genres such as rock, metal, punk, and indie.

Nefertiti: a pub and club that offers a jazz and soul feel. You may discover a bar area, a music hall, a dance floor, and a garden. You may appreciate music genres such as jazz, blues, soul, and funk.

You may also locate live music venues that showcase concerts and events from local and worldwide performers. Some of the popular places are:

The Gothenburg Music Hall is one of the best music venues in Scandinavia, with superb acoustics and architecture. It is the home of the Gothenburg Symphony Orchestra, one of Sweden's oldest and most prominent orchestras. It also features performances by various classical, jazz, pop, rock, and folk musicians.

The Gothenburg City Theatre is one of Sweden's biggest and most contemporary theatres, with four stages and a capacity for over 1,000 people. It provides a broad selection of plays, musicals, comedies, dramas, and children's programs. It also hosts events like the Gothenburg Theatre Festival and the Gothenburg Dance Festival.

The Pustervik: one of the most popular and adaptable venues in Gothenburg, with two stages and a capacity for over 800 people. It presents performances by local and worldwide performers from diverse genres such as rock, pop, indie, hip-hop, electronic, and folk. It also holds events such as comedy evenings, poetry slams, quiz nights, and flea markets.

The Avenyn Boulevard is a terrific area to have fun at night. You can discover pubs and clubs appealing to moods and music inclinations. You may also locate live music venues that showcase concerts and events from local and worldwide performers. Whether searching for a calm drink, a vibrant dance, or exhilarating entertainment, you can find something that will fit your taste on Avenyn Boulevard.

Magasinsgatan Street and the design stores

Magasinsgatan is one of the most stylish streets in Gothenburg, where you can find a range of design boutiques, cafés, restaurants, and pubs. Magasinsgatan is in the middle of the city, between Kungstorget and Vallgatan. The street was formerly a warehouse neighborhood but has become a bustling and creative center for local and international designers, artists, and entrepreneurs.

Magasinsgatan is where you may find fresh and distinctive things, from apparel and accessories to furniture and art. Whether you are searching for a present, a memento, or a treat for yourself, you will find something to fit your taste and budget at Magasinsgatan. Here are some of the attractions of Magasinsgatan Street and the design shops:

Grandpa: Grandpa is a lifestyle shop that offers apparel, accessories, books, periodicals, and home décor from Scandinavian and worldwide brands. Grandpa also conducts events, seminars, and exhibits promoting the newest fashion, design, and culture trends and skills. Grandpa is a location where you may get excellent things with a personal touch and a sense of fun.

Artilleriet: Artilleriet is a design shop that offers furniture, lighting, textiles, ceramics, and accessories from both classic and modern designers. Artilleriet also provides interior design services and consulting for private and public venues. Artilleriet is a site where you may discover inspiration and beauty for your home.

Nudie Jeans: Nudie Jeans is a denim brand launched in Gothenburg in 2001. Nudie Jeans is noted for its high-quality jeans constructed from organic cotton and unique design and fit. Nudie Jeans also provides repair services, recycling programs, and social responsibility activities that try to lessen the environmental effect of denim manufacture. Nudie Jeans is a location where you may get jeans that are more than simply garments.

Floramor & Krukatös: Floramor & Krukatös is a flower store that offers fresh flowers, plants, pots, vases, and accessories. Floramor & Krukatös also make bouquets, arrangements, and decorations for weddings, parties, and other events. Floramor & Krukatös is a site where you may discover flowers that are more than simply flowers.

Da Matteo: Da Matteo is a coffee roastery and bakery that offers coffee beans, bread, pastries, sandwiches, salads, and cakes. Da Matteo also sells coffee drinks, tea, juice, beer, wine, and cocktails in its pleasant café. Da Matteo is a location where you may obtain coffee that is more than simply coffee.

To end this chapter, Magasinsgatan is a street where you can discover various design businesses that provide unique and excellent items, from apparel and furniture to flowers and coffee. Magasinsgatan is a street where you may appreciate the ambiance, innovation, and variety of Gothenburg's design and retail sector. This chapter has provided valuable information and advice on arranging your trip to Magasinsgatan and making the most of your stay.

The Saluhallen market hall and the delicatessen stalls

Gothenburg is a city with a fantastic culinary culture where you can discover delectable specialties from all over the globe. One of the greatest venues to experience it is the Saluhallen market hall, the largest indoor market in town. Here you can discover spices, coffee, cheese, fruit, and other items from local and foreign sellers. You may also dine at one of the restaurants or cafés within the market hall or take away some food for later. Here are some reasons to visit the Saluhallen market hall and the delicatessen vendors.

The history of the market hall

The Saluhallen market hall was established in 1889 as a reaction to the increased need for fresh food in Gothenburg. The market hall was created by Hans Hedlund, a notable architect who worked on other structures in Gothenburg, such as the City Hall and the Fish Church. The market hall features a neo-Renaissance design, with a brick front, arched windows, and a clock tower.

The market hall has been restored numerous times, yet it has always kept its unique beauty and character. Today, the market hall is home to roughly 40 businesses and places to dine, providing a diverse variety of items and cuisines.

The diversity of the delicatessen booths

The Saluhallen market hall is a heaven for food enthusiasts, with its range of delicatessen vendors that cater to varied tastes and preferences. You may get anything from Swedish staples, such as meatballs, herring, and cheese, to unusual delicacies like sushi, falafel, and curry. You may also discover organic, vegetarian, and vegan choices.

Some of the most popular delicatessen booths in the Saluhallen market hall are:

Chocolate from Ahlgrens: A confectionery shop that has operated for over 30 years, delivering high-quality chocolate from major producers. You may also get licorice, marzipan, and gift boxes.

Little Italy Alfredo: A restaurant that provides freshly cooked pasta, pizza pieces, and gelato. You may also get Italian delights like cheese, ham, and olive oil.

Annie's Tea House: A business specializing in Boba tea, a sweet tea-based drink with flavored tapioca pearls. You may also get hand-picked Oolong tea from Taiwan.

Gateau: A bakery that offers cakes, pastries, biscuits, and bread baked with genuine butter and sourdough. You may also get tarts with varied layers and flavors.

Holmgren: A meat store that sells game, meat products, poultry, and steaks, with personal and professional service.

Fiskdisken: A fish store and restaurant that offers seasonal delicacies from sea and lake, such as oysters, mussels, scallops, and salmon. You may also get soup and ready-made meals.

How to get there

The Saluhallen market hall is in Kungstorget Square in the heart of Gothenburg. You may reach there by public transport, by bike or by foot.

By public transport: You may take tram number 1, 2, or 9 to Kungsportsplatsen station or tram number 3 or 4 to Domkyrkan stop. You may walk to the market hall in a few minutes.

By bike: You may hire a bike from one of the numerous stations in Gothenburg and pedal to Kungstorget Square. There are bike racks where you may keep your bike near the market hall.

By foot: You can stroll to Kungstorget Square from the major sights in Gothenburg, such as the Fish Church, the Art Museum, or the Liseberg Amusement Park.

When to go

The Saluhallen Market Hall is open all year round. However, it has varying opening hours depending on the day of the week. You may verify them on their website or phone them before you go.

- Monday-Friday: 9:00-18:00
- Saturday: 9:00-16:00

- Sunday: Closed

The ideal time to visit the Saluhallen market hall is in the morning or early afternoon when it is less crowded and more exciting. You may also visit there at lunchtime when you can discover several choices for a fast and good meal.

This chapter has given you a glimpse of the Saluhallen market hall and the delicatessen booths in Gothenburg, where you can discover a broad selection of goods and cuisines from local and foreign vendors. Saluhallen is a place to taste, smell and appreciate the culinary culture of Gothenburg, with its variety, quality, and service. Whether searching for a snack, a meal, or a souvenir, you will find something to fit your palette and budget at Saluhallen.

The Backa Teater and the current performances

Suppose you are seeking a theatrical experience that is original, challenging, and inspirational. You should visit the Backa Teater, an autonomous section of the Gothenburg City theatrical, with its own house, ensemble, and artistic director. The Backa Teater is situated in the historic shipbuilding neighborhood of Gothenburg, in a disused factory renovated into a contemporary and large theatre. The main stage, with its 20 x 40 meters, is one of the largest black boxes in Europe, allowing for versatile and innovative staging.

The Backa Teater was created in 1978 to utilize theatre as an art form to inspire the younger generation and so shift the path toward a better world. Since then, the theatre has acquired a reputation for creating plays for a young audience that is both current and creative. The theatre features a collection of about 4 new shows each year, primarily based on freshly written or adapted texts, that address subjects such as identity, diversity, democracy, and human rights. The theatre also partners with other theatres, artists, and academics from Sweden and abroad, establishing cross-cultural and multidisciplinary initiatives. The Backa Teater has been rewarded with various prizes, nationally and internationally, and has attracted well-renowned directors and writers. Some of the most outstanding works of the Backa Teater are:

- King Matt the First, by Mattias Andersson, based on the book by Janusz Korczak, is a tale about a youngster who becomes king and seeks to improve his nation.

- Acts of Goodness, by Mattias Andersson, is based on conversations with individuals who have done good actions in difficult conditions.

- The Misfits, by Mattias Andersson, is based on the film by John Huston, depicting four lonely and disillusioned individuals in Nevada.

- Hierarchy of Needs, by Adel Darwish, based on Maslow's theory of human motivation, is a play about four individuals who meet in an elevator that becomes trapped.

- Happily Ever After, by Lars Melin, is based on fairy tales by Hans Christian Andersen, a drama that explores the clichés and standards of love stories.

The Backa Teater is open every day except Mondays, from 10 am to 6 pm (or until 8 pm on Wednesdays). The entry charge varies according to the production, but it is normally approximately 200 SEK for adults and 100 SEK for children (4-16 years old). You may purchase your tickets online or at the entrance.

The Backa Teater is situated in Lindholmen, near the Lindholmen Science Park and the Lindholmen Ferry Terminal. You may easily access there by public transport (bus or boat), by vehicle (parking provided), or by bike (bike racks available). You may also find a café within the theatre, where you can have a snack or a drink.

The Backa Teater is a location where you may witness current, controversial, and interesting theatre. It is a place where you see different viewpoints, question your ideas, and feel inspired.

CHAPTER 5

3-7 Days Itinerary in Gothenburg

Gothenburg is a city that provides a lot of attractions and activities for tourists, whether they stay for a weekend or a week. You may enjoy the city's culture, history, wildlife, and nightlife and explore its environs and the West Coast of Sweden. Here is a proposed plan for 3-7 days in Gothenburg, depending on how much time you have and what you are interested in.

Day 1: Discover the city center

On your first day in Gothenburg, you may get to know the city center and its important landmarks. You may start by visiting the Feskekörka, a fish market that looks like a cathedral, where you can purchase fresh seafood or have a snack at one of the eateries. Then, you may stroll to the Gothenburg City Museum, where you can learn about the city's history and witness the only Viking ship on show in Sweden.

Next, you may travel to the Maritime, a maritime museum that exhibits a variety of ships and submarines that you can board and explore. You may also appreciate the views of the

Göta River and the port from here. Afterward, you may go to the Gothenburg Opera House, a spectacular structure with opera, ballet, musicals, and concerts. You may attend a performance or take a guided tour of the building.

In the evening, you may wander down the Avenyn, the major avenue of Gothenburg, where you can discover some of the city's most famous and prominent stores, restaurants, pubs, and cafés. You may also observe some of the most renowned structures and landmarks of Gothenburg, such as the City Theatre, the Concert Hall, the Museum of Art, and the Poseidon statue.

Day 2: Explore additional museums and parks

On your second day in Gothenburg, you may visit additional museums and parks exhibiting the city's culture and environment. You might start by visiting the Gothenburg Museum of Art, where you can appreciate paintings by great painters like Rembrandt, Rubens, Picasso, Monet, and Munch. The museum also includes a great collection of Nordic art from the late 19th and early 20th centuries.

Next, you may visit the Scandinavium, an indoor arena that has held various athletic and entertainment events throughout the years. You may either attend a game or a performance or take a guided tour of the stadium. Then, you may travel to Liseberg amusement park, where you can have some fun on the rides and attractions for all ages. You may also have some food and drink at one of the numerous restaurants and cafés in the park.

Afterward, you may visit the Museum of Global Culture, where you can study civilizations across the globe and view a broad selection of objects on exhibit. You may also attend some of the seminars and activities hosted by the museum. Then, you may stroll to Linné Street, where you can discover some of the city's greatest street art and unusual businesses. You can also discover some of the city's top coffee shops, pubs, and restaurants here.

Finally, you may conclude your day at Gothenburg Botanical Garden, where you can observe more than 16 000 varieties of plants from all over the globe. You may also visit the greenhouses to observe tropical and subtropical flora. You may also enjoy some peace at one of the garden's numerous seats and picnic places.

Day 3: Visit Skansen Kronan and Haga

On your third day in Gothenburg, you may explore Skansen Kronan and Haga, two of the city's oldest and most picturesque neighborhoods. You might start by visiting Skansen Kronan, a castle erected in 1687 to safeguard Gothenburg against Danish assaults. You may trek up to the top of the hill where the castle sits and enjoy the panoramic views of the city. You may also visit the museum within the stronghold, where you can view various historical artifacts and weaponry.

Next, you may go to Haga, one of the oldest and most picturesque areas in Gothenburg, with its typical wooden buildings with stone foundations. Here, you may enjoy a comfortable and easygoing environment, with lots of shops, cafés, restaurants, and bars. You may also explore some of the attractions in Haga, such as:

The Haga Church is a neo-Gothic church that was erected in 1859 and has a lovely interior and stained glass windows.
The Haga Bathhouse is a public bathhouse that was erected in 1898 and has been restored to its original form. You may either plunge in the pools or relax in the sauna.

The Haga Nygata, the main street in Haga, is where you can find some of the greatest stores and cafés in the neighborhood. You may also taste the famed Haga bun, a huge cinnamon bun delicacy of Haga.

Day 4: Visit the archipelago

On your fourth day in Gothenburg, you may explore the archipelago, a series of islands off the coast of Gothenburg. You may take a ferry or boat excursion from the city center and visit some islands that offer diverse sights and activities. Some of the most popular islands are:

Styrsö, an island that boasts a lovely town with wooden buildings and gardens. You may also enjoy various hiking and bike paths on the island and view historical monuments like the Styrsö Church and the Styrsö Skäret Lighthouse.
Brännö is an island that offers a vibrant environment with music and dancing activities. You may also enjoy some swimming and sunbathing on the beaches and rocks on the island and view some wildlife, such as seals and birds.

Vrångö is an island with a natural reserve with unique flora and wildlife. You may also enjoy some fishing and kayaking on the island and explore some cultural sights like the Vrångö Museum and the Vrångö Chapel.

Day 5: Visit Gothenburg's environs

On your fifth day in Gothenburg, you may see some of the sites in Gothenburg's environs. You may hire a vehicle or take a bus or train from the city center and tour some destinations that provide diverse sensations and views. Some of the most popular destinations are:

Marstrand is a beach village noted for its sailing and boating culture. You can also visit some of the attractions in Marstrand, such as the Marstrand Castle, a fortress that was built in 1658 and offers stunning views of the sea; the Carlsten Lighthouse, a lighthouse that was built in 1849 and has a museum inside; and the Marstrand Church, a church that was built in 1736 and has a beautiful altar painting.

Borås is a city recognized for its textile industry and street art. You can also visit some of the attractions in Borås, such as the Textile Museum, a museum that showcases the history and development of textile production in Borås; the Borås Zoo, a zoo that has more than 600 animals from different continents; and the No Limit Street Art Festival, a festival that features murals and sculptures by local and international artists.

Alingsås is a city recognized for its coffee culture and lights festival. You can also visit some of the attractions in Alingsås, such as the Alingsås Museum, a museum that displays the history and culture of Alingsås; the Nolhaga Park, a park that has a castle, a lake, and a playground; and the Lights in Alingsås Festival, a festival that features light installations and shows by local and international artists.

Day 6: Visit the West Coast

On your sixth day in Gothenburg, you may explore the West Coast, a location noted for its natural beauty and seafood. You may hire a vehicle or take a bus or train from Gothenburg and tour some cities and villages offering diverse sights and activities. Some of the most popular destinations are:

Smögen is a fishing community with a picturesque waterfront, wooden cottages, and boats. You can also enjoy some shopping and dining at the Smögenbryggan, a pier that has shops, restaurants, and cafes; some swimming and diving at the Smögen Hafvsbad, a beach resort that has a spa and a pool; and some hiking and biking at the Smögen Nature Reserve, a reserve that has trails and viewpoints.

Fjällbacka is a fishing hamlet with a lovely ambiance, cobblestone lanes, and stone buildings. You can also visit some of the attractions in Fjällbacka, such as the Fjällbacka Church, a church that was built in 1627 and has a wooden tower; the Ingrid Bergman Square, a square that honors the famous actress who spent her summers in Fjällbacka; and the Kungsklyftan, a gorge that has huge rocks and was used as a filming location for some movies.

Grebbestad is a fishing community noted for its oysters and festivals. You may also enjoy some activities in Grebbestad, such as oyster tasting, oyster safari, oyster opening competition, and oyster festival; some kayaking and sailing on the sea; and some golfing at the TanumStrand Golf Club, a golf club that includes an 18-hole course.

Day 7: Visit Trollhättan and Vänersborg

On your seventh day in Gothenburg, you may explore Trollhättan and Vänersborg, two towns on Lake Vänern, the biggest lake in Sweden. You may hire a vehicle or take a bus or a train from Gothenburg and visit some of the sites and activities in these locations. Some of the more popular ones are:

The Trollhättan Falls and Locks, where you can view the stunning waterfalls and locks that control the water level of the Göta River. You can also visit some of the museums nearby, such as the Saab Car Museum, which displays the history and development of Saab cars; the Innovatum Science Center, which offers interactive exhibits and experiments on science and technology; and the Olidan Power Station Museum, which shows how electricity is produced from water.

The Vänersborg Museum, where you may learn about the history and culture of Vänersborg and its surrounds. You may also view certain collections of art, natural history, archaeology, anthropology, and music. You can also visit some of the exhibitions that are organized by the museum, such as the Tresticklan National Park Exhibition, which showcases the nature and wildlife of the park; the Carl Larsson Exhibition, which features paintings by the famous Swedish artist; and the Elsa Beskow Exhibition, which features illustrations by the famous Swedish children's book author.

The Halleberg and Hunneberg Plateaus, where you may enjoy some hiking and bicycling on the routes that give stunning views of Lake Vänern and the surrounding woodlands. You can also visit some of the attractions on the plateaus, such as the Royal Hunt Museum, which displays the history and tradition of hunting on the plateaus; the Vänersborgs Art Gallery, which exhibits works by local and regional artists; and the Ecopark Halle-Hunneberg, which offers guided tours and activities on ecology and conservation.

This is an itinerary for 3-7 days in Gothenburg, depending on how much time you have and what you are interested in. You may change it according to your interests and requirements or mix and match the various days and activities. You may also find additional information and recommendations on the official website of Gothenburg Tourism.

Gothenburg is a city that provides a lot of attractions and activities for tourists, whether they stay for a weekend or a week. You may enjoy the city's culture, history, wildlife, and nightlife and explore its environs and the West Coast of Sweden. Gothenburg is a city that will surprise you and make you fall in love with it.

CHAPTER 6

Accommodation and Dining

Gothenburg is a city that provides many alternatives for lodging and restaurants, whether you are searching for comfort, luxury, flair, or affordability. You may discover anything from hotels and hostels to flats and cottages, from Swedish and Scandinavian to foreign and exotic cuisines. You may also locate venues that cater to certain requirements and interests, such as family-friendly, eco-friendly, or pet-friendly. No matter where you stay or what you eat, you will love the quality and hospitality of Gothenburg.

In this chapter, we will lead you through some of the greatest neighborhoods and venues to enjoy lodging and eating in Gothenburg. We will show you where to discover the city's most acceptable and convenient hotels, hostels, flats, and cottages. We will also show you where to discover the city's most tasty and varied restaurants, cafés, bars, and pubs. We will also provide you with some advice and suggestions on how to make the most of your lodging and eating experience in Gothenburg. Whether you are seeking a comfortable bed & breakfast, a magnificent hotel suite, a classic Swedish smörgåsbord, or a spicy Thai curry, you can find it in Gothenburg. Let's get started!

The top hotels and hostels in Gothenburg for varied budgets and interests

Gothenburg is a city that provides many alternatives for lodging, whether you are searching for comfort, luxury, flair, or affordability. You may discover anything from hotels and hostels to flats and cottages, from Swedish and Scandinavian to foreign and exotic styles. You may also locate venues that cater to certain requirements and interests, such as family-friendly, eco-friendly, or pet-friendly. No matter where you stay, you will appreciate the quality and warmth of Gothenburg.

In this sub chapter, we will lead you through some of the greatest hotels and hostels in Gothenburg that provide a variety of facilities and services to make your stay in the city memorable. We will show you where to discover the city's most acceptable and convenient hotels and hostels, depending on your budget and desire. We will also provide advice and suggestions on making the most of your hotel experience in Gothenburg. Whether you are seeking a nice bed & breakfast, a magnificent hotel suite, a contemporary hostel dorm, or a huge apartment, you can find it in Gothenburg.

Budget accommodation in Gothenburg

If you are traveling on a limited budget or seeking a friendly and lively environment, consider staying at one of the numerous hostels in Gothenburg. Hostels are affordable and provide a range of amenities and services, such as free Wi-Fi, communal kitchens, common spaces, laundry rooms, lockers, bike rentals, and more. You may also meet other travelers and attend some of the events and activities that hostels arrange, such as bar crawls, movie evenings, game nights, and excursions. Hostels normally provide both dormitory rooms and private rooms, so you may select the amount of privacy and comfort that fits you best.

Some of the nicest hostels in Gothenburg are:

SpotOn Hostel & Sportsbar is a hostel in Gothenburg, barely 150 meters from the south entrance of Liseberg Amusement Park. The nearest tram stop is about a 2-minute walk away. The rooms offer air conditioning and complimentary WiFi. Bathrooms are either private or shared. At SpotOn Hostel & Sportsbar, you can discover a bar and restaurant providing internationally-inspired meals. A buffet and a la carte menu for the evening are given at lunch. Shared amenities include a kitchen and a shared lounge. The hostel is 850 meters from the Swedish Exhibition and Congress Centre, 1.1 km from Scandinavium Arena, and 2 km from Ullevi Stadium. Gothenburg Central Station is 2.5 miles distant.

Backpackers Göteborg is a hostel in a calm residential neighborhood near Slottsskogen Park. It offers free Wi-Fi, free parking, free coffee/tea, free pasta/rice/oatmeal/spices/sauce/oil/vinegar/sugar/salt/pepper/milk/butter/jam/cheese/bread/cereals/yogurt/eggs/fruits/vegetables/cakes/biscuits/candy/chocolate/nuts/dried fruits/popcorn/crisps/soda/juice/beer/wine (yes, all free!), free laundry/detergent/softener/dryer/iron/board/hangers (yes, all free!), free lockers/safes/luggage storage, and more.

It also contains a garden, a patio, a grilling area, a sauna, a games room, and a library. It provides both dormitory accommodations and individual rooms with communal or private bathrooms. It is 2 kilometers from Avenyn Avenue, 2.5 km from Liseberg Amusement Park, and 3 km from Gothenburg Central Station.

Slottsskogens Youth Hostel is a hostel that is situated in Slottsskogen Park, surrounded by vegetation and animals. It provides free Wi-Fi, free parking, free coffee/tea, a free breakfast buffet, free linen/towels (yep, everything is free!), and more. It also features a kitchen, a dining room, a lounge, a TV room, a laundry room, and a sauna. It provides both dormitory accommodations and individual rooms with communal or private bathrooms. It is 1 km from the Haga neighborhood, 1.5 km from Avenyn Boulevard, and 2 km from the Gothenburg City Museum.

Mid-range accommodation in Gothenburg

Suppose you seek a pleasant and convenient lodging choice without breaking the bank. In that case, consider staying at one of the numerous hotels in Gothenburg that provide fantastic value for money. These hotels provide facilities and services, such as Wi-Fi, breakfast, TV, minibar, hairdryer, and more. You may also select hotels that provide some additional services, such as a gym, pool, spa, or restaurant. You may locate these hotels in various sections of the city, such as:

The city center: the heart of Gothenburg, where you can find some of the city's most prominent and handy hotels.

You may appreciate the vicinity of the major attractions, shopping, restaurants, pubs, and transit connections. Some of the popular mid-range hotels in the city center are:

The Hotel Royal is a hotel that is located in a historic structure from 1852. It is the oldest hotel in Gothenburg and has been managed by the same family for four generations. It includes about 70 rooms and suites with traditional and exquisite décor. It also offers a lobby bar and a breakfast room. It is near the Stora Saluhallen, the Gothenburg City Theatre, and the Gothenburg Concert Hall.

The Hotel Opera is a hotel near the Göteborg Opera House. It offers about 200 rooms and suites with contemporary and elegant designs. It also features a gym, a pool, a spa, and a restaurant. It is near the Lilla Bommen, the Nordstan Shopping Center, and the Gothenburg Central Station.

The Hotel Riverton hotel is positioned by the Rosenlund Canal, with a view of the port and the city. It offers about 180 rooms and suites in a modern and friendly style. It also features a sky bar, a lounge, and a restaurant. It is situated near the Feskekörka fish market, the City Museum, and the Haga neighborhood.

The Majorna-Linné district: a fashionable and bohemian region in Gothenburg, where you can discover some of the city's most unique and unusual hotels. You may enjoy the ambiance of the district, with its cafés, galleries, markets, and festivals. Some of the popular mid-range hotels in the Majorna-Linné neighborhood are:

The Hotel Vasa is a hotel that is located in a former school building from 1886. It includes around 40 rooms and suites with colorful and unique designs. It also offers a breakfast area, a sauna, and a garden. It is near Slottsskogen Park, the Gothenburg Natural History Museum, and the Skansen Kronan.

The Hotel Vanilla is a hotel housed in a historic structure from 1786. It includes about 30 rooms and suites with traditional and exquisite décor. It also offers a breakfast area, a library, and a patio. It is near the Stora Saluhallen, the Gothenburg City Theatre, and the Gothenburg Concert Hall.

The Hotel Flora is a hotel housed in a former warehouse from 1900. It offers about 60 rooms and suites with contemporary and minimalist decor. It also boasts a rooftop patio, a courtyard garden, and a café. It is near the Feskekörka fish market, the Haga neighborhood, and the Skansen Kronan.

Luxury accommodation in Gothenburg

If you are searching for a premium and exclusive lodging choice, consider staying at one of the numerous hotels in Gothenburg that provide high service and comfort. These hotels provide a selection of facilities and services, such as Wi-Fi, breakfast, TV, minibar, hairdryer, bathrobe, slippers, and more. You may also select hotels that provide additional services, such as a gym, pool, spa, restaurant, or bar. You may locate these hotels in various sections of the city, such as:

The city center: the heart of Gothenburg, where you can find some of the city's most prominent and handy hotels. You may appreciate the vicinity of the major attractions, shopping, restaurants, pubs, and transit connections. Some of the popular luxury hotels in the city center are:

The Dorsia Hotel & Restaurant is influenced by the Art Nouveau style of the early 20th century. It contains about 30 rooms and suites with magnificent and spectacular designs. It also contains a restaurant, a bar, a library, and a patio. It is near Avenyn Avenue, the City Museum, and the Kronhuset.

The Upper House is a hotel situated on the Gothia Towers' upper floors. It offers approximately 50 rooms and suites with contemporary and exquisite styles. It also offers a spa, a gym, a pool, and a restaurant. It gives a wonderful perspective of the city and the waterfront. It is near the Liseberg Amusement Park, the Museum of World Culture, and the Universeum Science Center.

The Avalon Hotel is a hotel that is created according to the principles of Feng Shui. It offers about 100 rooms and suites with trendy and harmonious decor. It also boasts a rooftop pool, a sauna, and a restaurant. It is near the Stora Saluhallen, the Gothenburg City Theatre, and the Gothenburg Concert Hall.

The Majorna-Linné district: a fashionable and bohemian region in Gothenburg, where you can discover some of the city's most unique and unusual hotels. You may enjoy the district's ambiance, with its cafés, galleries, markets, and festivals. Some of the popular luxury hotels in the Majorna-Linné neighborhood are:

The Hotel Pigalle is a hotel inspired by the Parisian Belle Époque period. It includes about 40 rooms and suites with romantic and colorful designs. It also features a rooftop patio, a cocktail bar, and a restaurant. It is near the Stora Saluhallen, the Gothenburg City Theatre, and the Gothenburg Concert Hall.

The Hotel Bellora is a hotel that the Italian Riviera inspires. It includes around 90 rooms and suites with bright and inviting designs. It also offers a rooftop patio, a bar, and a restaurant. It is near Avenyn Avenue, the City Museum, and the Kronhuset.

The Hotel Flora is a hotel housed in a former warehouse from 1900. It offers about 60 rooms and suites with contemporary and minimalist decor. It also boasts a rooftop patio, a courtyard garden, and a café. It is near the Feskekörka fish market, the Haga neighborhood, and the Skansen Kronan.

Gothenburg is a city that provides many alternatives for lodging, whether you are searching for comfort, luxury, flair, or affordability. You may discover anything from hotels and hostels to flats and cottages, from Swedish and Scandinavian to foreign and exotic styles. You may also locate venues that cater to certain requirements and interests, such as family-friendly, eco-friendly, or pet-friendly. No matter where you stay, you will appreciate the quality and warmth of Gothenburg.

The Best Restaurants and Cafés in Gothenburg for various cuisines and events

Gothenburg is a city that boasts a rich and diversified food scene, where you can discover restaurants and cafés that appeal to various tastes, budgets, and events. Whether you are seeking classic Swedish meals, cosmopolitan tastes, or contemporary locations, you will find something to satisfy your palette in Gothenburg. Here are some of the greatest restaurants and cafés in Gothenburg for various cuisines and events, including their website and location.

Swedish cuisine

If you wish to experience some of the iconic Swedish meals, such as meatballs, herring, or smörgåsbord, you may visit some restaurants specializing in Swedish cuisine. Some of the finest ones are:

Sjömagasinet is a Michelin-starred restaurant that offers seafood and seasonal meals in a historic structure on the port. You may enjoy the views of the sea and the boats from the dining room or the patio. Website: sjomagasinet.se Address: Adolf Edelsvärds gata 5, 414 51 Gothenburg

Kometen is a modest and stylish restaurant that has been serving Swedish classics since 1934. You may find entrees such as beef Rydberg, veal liver, fried herring on the menu, and sweets such as apple pie or crème brûlée. Website: restaurangkometen.se Address: Vasagatan 58, 411 37 Gothenburg.

Smaka is a trendy and informal restaurant that provides a range of Swedish meals with a twist. You may select from delicacies such as elk meatballs, smoked salmon salad, mushroom risotto, and vegan and gluten-free alternatives. Website: smakagoteborg.se Address: Vasaplatsen 3, 411 34 Gothenburg.

International cuisine

If you want to try cuisines from across the globe, you may visit some restaurants that provide foreign food. Some of the finest ones are:

Puta Madre is a Mexican restaurant that delivers genuine and spicy meals with a contemporary flair. You may discover delicacies like tacos, burritos, enchiladas, ceviche on the menu, drinks, and tequila. Website: putamadre.se Address: Magasinsgatan 3A, 411 18 Gothenburg.

Hello, Monkey is an Asian fusion restaurant that provides foods from Thailand, Vietnam, Japan, and China. You may discover delicacies such as pad thai, pho, sushi, dim sum on the menu, and sake and beer. Website: hellomonkey.se Address: Magasinsgatan 26B, 411 18 Gothenburg.

Barabicu is a South American restaurant that offers grilled meat and fish with unusual sauces and sides. You may discover meals such as picanha steak, grilled octopus, or ceviche on the menu, as well as drinks and wine. Website: barabicu.se Address: Parkgatan 13A, 411 38 Gothenburg

Trendy places

Suppose you want to explore some of the fashionable sites popular with residents and tourists. In that case, you may visit some restaurants and cafés that provide a stylish and energetic ambiance. Some of the finest ones are:

Koka is a Michelin-starred restaurant that serves innovative and seasonal cuisine focused on local foods. You may pick from numerous tasting menus highlighting West Sweden's finest products and tastes. Website: koka.se Address: Viktoriagatan 12A, 411 25 Gothenburg.

Fiskbar 17 is a seafood restaurant that provides a relaxed and friendly environment with a nautical feel. You may discover foods such as fish & chips, lobster rolls, seafood platters on the menu, and beer and wine. Website: fiskbar17.se Address: Rosenlundsgatan 17, 411 20 Gothenburg.

Brewers Beer Pub is a craft beer pub that provides a broad range of beers from local and worldwide brewers. You may also eat some pizza, sandwiches, or snacks to go with your drink. Website: brewersbeerbar.se Address: Tredje Långgatan 8, 413 03 Gothenburg.

Cafes

If you wish to have coffee, tea, or cake, you may visit some cafes that provide a comfortable and quiet setting. Some of the finest ones are:

Da Matteo is a coffee roastery and café that provides high-quality coffee and excellent pastries. You may also purchase some coffee beans or equipment to take home. Website: damatteo.se Address: Magasinsgatan 17A, 411 18 Gothenburg.

Cum Pane is a bakery and café that sells organic bread and pastries prepared with sourdough and natural ingredients. You may also eat some sandwiches, salads, or soups for lunch. Website: cumpane.se Address: Haga Nygata 9, 413 01 Gothenburg.

Cafe Husaren is a cafe that provides the famed Haga bun, a huge cinnamon bun that is a specialty of Gothenburg. You may also enjoy various delicacies like cardamom buns, chocolate balls, or carrot cake. Website: cafehusaren.se Address: Haga Nygata 28, 413 01 Gothenburg.

This is a list of some of the greatest restaurants and cafés in Gothenburg for various cuisines and events, including their website and location. You can find additional information on the official website of Gothenburg Tourism.

Gothenburg is a city that boasts a rich and diversified food scene, where you can discover restaurants and cafés that appeal to various tastes, budgets, and events. Whether you are seeking classic Swedish meals, cosmopolitan tastes, or contemporary locations, you will find something to satisfy your palette in Gothenburg. Gothenburg is a city that will thrill you and make you eager for more.

CHAPTER 7: Practical Information.

Visa requirements for visiting Gothenburg

Gothenburg is a city that welcomes travelers from all over the globe, but depending on your country and the reason for your stay, you may require a visa to enter Sweden. A visa is permission to travel to and remain in a country for a specified duration. Here are some of the visa requirements for visiting Gothenburg, depending on the most prevalent forms of travel.

Tourist visa

If you are visiting Gothenburg as a tourist, for leisure or sightseeing, you may or may not require a visa, depending on your citizenship. Sweden is part of the Schengen area, which includes 26 European nations that have eliminated passport and border restrictions at their shared borders. If you are a citizen of one of these countries, you may travel to Gothenburg without a visa if your stay is at most 90 days in any 180 days.

If you are a non-EU country citizen with a visa exemption agreement with the Schengen region, you may also travel to

Gothenburg without a visa under the same restrictions. These nations include Australia, Canada, Japan, New Zealand, South Korea, the United States, and many more. You can view the entire list of visa-exempt countries here.

If you are a citizen of a non-EU country that does not have a visa exemption agreement with the Schengen region, you will need to apply for a Schengen visa to visit Gothenburg. A Schengen visa permits you to remain in the Schengen region for up to 90 days in any 180-day period for tourism or other short-term reasons. You may view the entire list of countries whose residents need a Schengen visa here.

To apply for a Schengen visa, you must submit an application form and accompanying papers to the Swedish embassy or consulate in your residency. You must also pay a visa fee and give biometric data (fingerprints and pictures). You should apply for your visa at least 15 days before your anticipated travel date. You may discover additional information and criteria for Schengen visa applications here.

Business visa

If you are visiting Gothenburg for business activities, such as attending meetings, conferences, trade fairs, or training courses, you may or may not require a visa, depending on your citizenship and the length of your stay. The same regulations and criteria for tourist visas also apply to business visas. However, you may need to produce additional documentation to show the purpose and nature of your business travel, such as an invitation letter from your Swedish partner or host organization or evidence of registration for an event.

Work visa

Suppose you are visiting Gothenburg for work reasons, such as employment by a Swedish firm or organization or being self-employed in Sweden. In that case, you will require a work visa to enter and remain in Sweden. A work permit is distinct from a visa and permits you to work and reside in Sweden for over 90 days. You will also need to apply for a residence permit card, an identification document indicating that you have authorization to remain in Sweden.

You must submit an application form and accompanying papers to the Swedish Migration Agency to apply for a work permit and a residence permit card. You must also pay an application fee and furnish biometric data (fingerprints and pictures). You should apply for your work permit before you arrive in Sweden. You may discover additional information and requirements for work permit applications here.

Study visa

Suppose you are visiting Gothenburg for study reasons, such as enrolling in a university or college course or participating in an exchange program or internship. In that case, you will require a residence visa for studies to enter and remain in Sweden. A residence permit for studies is distinct from a visa and permits you to study and remain in Sweden for more than 90 days. You will also need to apply for a residence permit card, an identification document indicating that you have authorization to remain in Sweden.

You must submit an application form and accompanying papers to the Swedish Migration Agency to apply for a residence permit for studies and a residence permit card. You must also pay an application fee and furnish biometric data (fingerprints and pictures). You should apply for your residence permit as soon as possible after getting your acceptance letter from your Swedish university or institution. You may discover additional information and requirements for residency permit applications here.

Other forms of visas

There may be additional sorts of visas that fit your circumstances or purpose of travel better than the ones indicated above, for example, if you are visiting Gothenburg as part of an official delegation or mission from another country or organization; if you are visiting Gothenburg as a journalist, artist, or performer; if you are visiting Gothenburg for medical treatment or humanitarian reasons; or if you are visiting Gothenburg as a family member or partner of a Swedish citizen or resident.

The following countries are visa-free when visiting Gothenburg since they are members of the Schengen region or have a visa exemption agreement with the Schengen area: Albania

- Andorra
- Antigua and Barbuda
- Argentina

- Australia
- Austria
- Bahamas
- Barbados
- Belgium
- Bosnia and Herzegovina
- Brazil
- Brunei
- Bulgaria
- Canada
- Chile
- Colombia
- Costa Rica
- Croatia
- Cyprus
- Czech Republic
- Denmark
- Dominica
- El Salvador
- Estonia
- Finland
- France
- Georgia
- Germany
- Greece
- Grenada
- Guatemala
- Honduras
- Hong Kong (SAR China)

Passport and travel documents

Whether you require a visa or not, you will need a valid passport and travel papers to enter and depart Sweden. Your passport must be:

1. Issued less than 10 years before the day you enter Sweden (check the 'date of issue)

2. Valid for at least 3 months after the day you want to leave Sweden (check the 'expiry date')

3. You should also ensure that your passport is stamped when you enter or depart the Schengen region via Sweden, as this will allow border guards to verify that you comply with the 90-day visa-free restriction for short visits in the Schengen area.

Conclusion

We hope this chapter has been useful and instructive and has addressed any questions and worries regarding visiting Gothenburg. We also hope it has motivated you to plan your vacation to Gothenburg and enjoy its sights and activities. Gothenburg is a city that greets you with open arms and a warm welcome. We wish you a safe and pleasurable travel to Gothenburg.

Health and Safety Advice for Traveling to Gothenburg

Gothenburg is a city that is typically secure and healthy for tourists, but it is always advisable to take some measures and be aware of the possible hazards and problems. In this chapter, we will present you with some health and safety information for going to Gothenburg, covering subjects such as:

- COVID-19 regulations and recommendations
- Vaccinations and medical services
- Crime and security
- Natural calamities and weather

Emergency contacts and essential resources

This sub chapter will help you plan your trip and enjoy your time in Gothenburg.

COVID-19 regulations and recommendations

As of July 2023, Sweden has lifted most of its COVID-19 limitations, although certain limits remain. Here are some of the current restrictions and suggestions that you should follow while going to Gothenburg:

All passengers entering Sweden are expected to follow the instructions that apply—how to protect yourself and others — COVID-19 guidelines. Read about COVID-19 in other languages.

Suppose you are going from a country outside the EU/EEA or the UK. In that case, you may need to provide a negative COVID-19 test result obtained at most 48 hours before arrival or evidence of immunization or recovery. Check the current entrance requirements before your travel. Travel to and stay in Sweden or visit Sweden.

If you suffer signs of COVID-19, such as fever, cough, or loss of taste or smell, you should self-isolate and be tested as soon as possible. You may arrange a free test online or by phone at 1177. For guidance and aid in case of sickness, visit the website 1177.se: Collective information on COVID-19.

You should use a face mask while utilizing public transit, attending health care institutions, or when you cannot maintain a distance from people. You should also wash your hands regularly, avoid big gatherings, and remain home if you are unwell.

You should observe the operating hours and capacity restrictions of stores, restaurants, bars, museums, theatres, and other facilities. You should also observe these venues' cleanliness regulations and social distance requirements.

You should check the official websites of the destinations you plan to visit for the latest information and updates. Some locations may demand previous reservations or have additional limitations for visitors.

Vaccinations and medical services

Sweden offers good quality health care and medical services, but it is always wise to get travel insurance covering your medical bills in an emergency. Here are some of the immunizations and medical services that you should consider while visiting Gothenburg:

You should ensure you have all the usual vaccines advised by your home country, such as measles-mumps-rubella (MMR), diphtheria-tetanus-pertussis (DTP), polio, hepatitis A and B, and influenza.

You may also require certain extra vaccines depending on your trip intentions, such as tick-borne encephalitis (TBE) if you are planning to spend time in woodland or rural regions or rabies if you are going to be in touch with animals. Consult your doctor or a travel clinic before your trip.

You should pack adequate prescription medicine for your vacation, as well as a copy of your prescription and a note from your doctor outlining your illness and treatment. You should also pack some over-the-counter medicine for common conditions, such as painkillers, antihistamines, antidiarrheals, and rehydration salts.

If you require medical assistance in Gothenburg, you may visit one of the numerous healthcare facilities (vårdcentraler) or pharmacies (apotek) throughout the city. You may also call 1177 for health advice or 112 for emergencies. Depending on your insurance or citizenship status, you may need to pay a price for certain services. For additional information about health care in Sweden, check the website 1177.se: Health care in Sweden.

Crime and security

Gothenburg is a reasonably calm and quiet city, yet it is not immune to crime and violence. You should take care and common sense while traveling in Gothenburg, particularly at night or in new places. Here are some of the criminal and security problems that you should be aware of while visiting Gothenburg:

Pickpockets are prevalent in tourist areas and during festivals. They frequently operate in teams, where one distracts you while another grabs your goods. Be extra vigilant at railway terminals and busy locations. Only bring a little cash or valuables with you. Keep your stuff near to you and safe at all times.

Scams, such as fraudulent tickets, illegal taxis, or overpriced services, are widespread in tourist locations. You should always examine the pricing and the validity of the service before you pay. You should also avoid exchanging money on the street or at unauthorized sites. Use only licensed cabs, banks, or ATMs.

Muggings and robberies are infrequent, yet they do happen. You should avoid walking alone at night or in secluded regions. You should also avoid confrontation with inebriated or violent persons. If you are assaulted, do not struggle and give up your belongings. Then notify the police as soon as possible.

Terrorism is a minimal danger in Gothenburg, although it is not impossible. You should be attentive and watchful in public and report suspicious activities or conduct to the police. You should also avoid engaging in public protests or political rallies. Check the latest security advisories before your journey—Sweden travel tips.

Natural catastrophes and weather

Gothenburg is a city prone to weather-related floods produced by severe rainfall, flooded rivers, and high sea levels, particularly during storm surges. Today heavy rains are the most danger inflicting the greatest impacts. You should verify the weather prediction before your journey and follow the directions of the local authorities in case of an emergency. Here are some of the natural catastrophes and weather situations that you should be prepared for while going to Gothenburg:

Floods are frequent in Gothenburg, particularly in low-lying regions near the river or the sea. They may cause damage to property, infrastructure, and transportation. You should avoid driving or walking over flooded roads or bridges. You should also migrate to higher ground in a flood-prone location.

Storms are common in Gothenburg, particularly in fall and winter. They may bring severe winds, heavy rain, snow, hail, thunder, and lightning. They may also create power outages, fallen trees, and traffic problems. You should remain inside and away from windows during a storm. You should also secure your things and have a torch and a radio ready.

Snow and ice are prevalent in Gothenburg, particularly in winter. They may make the roadways and walkways slippery and unsafe. They may also impact public transit and airport operations. You should dress warmly and have suitable footwear while going outdoors. You should also check the road conditions and the transit timetables before you go.

Emergency contacts and valuable resources

Gothenburg is a city that has a well-developed emergency response system and a variety of beneficial tools for tourists. You should always have some emergency contacts and essential resources accessible while going to Gothenburg, such as:

• 112: the universal emergency number for police, fire, ambulance, or rescue services.

• 1177: the health advice hotline for non-emergency medical concerns or queries.

• +46 771 14 14 14: the tourist information number for Gothenburg.

- +46 31 368 42 00: the number for the British Consulate in Gothenburg.

- +46 8 783 53 00: the number for the US Embassy in Stockholm.

- https://www.goteborg.com/en/: the official website for Gothenburg tourism.

- https://www.vasttrafik.se/en/: the official website for public transportation in Gothenburg.

- https://www.folkhalsomyndigheten.se/the-public-health-agency-of-sweden/communicable-disease-control/covid-19/: the official website for COVID-19 information in Sweden.

Gothenburg is a city that is typically secure and healthy for tourists, but it is always advisable to take some measures and be aware of the possible hazards and problems. We hope this chapter has given you some health and safety information when coming to Gothenburg, including COVID-19 legislation and recommendations, vaccines and medical services, crime and security, natural catastrophes and weather, emergency contacts, and valuable resources.

Currency and Banking Choices in Gothenburg

Gothenburg is a city that provides a number of alternatives for money and banking based on your tastes, requirements, and budget. Whether you prefer cash, cards, or mobile payments, you will find something to fit your taste and convenience in Gothenburg. Here are some of the currency and banking possibilities in Gothenburg:

Currency in Gothenburg

The official currency of Gothenburg is the Swedish krona (SEK), which is split into 100 öre. However, the öre coins have been phased out, and any things priced in öre are rounded up to the closest krona. The krona coins are available in 1, 2, 5, and 10 denominations. The banknotes are produced in denominations of 20, 50, 100, 200, 500, and 1,000 kronor.

Gothenburg is not part of the eurozone, meaning you cannot pay with euros or other currencies than SEK in cash. If you attempt to pay with foreign money, you will likely obtain a bad conversion rate or be denied completely. Therefore, converting your money to SEK before or upon arriving in Gothenburg is best.

Currency Exchange in Gothenburg

There are various options to convert your money to SEK in Gothenburg. One alternative is to utilize a currency exchange office, such as Forex/X-change, Tavex, Change Group, Ria, or another currency exchange office. These offices are placed in different sites in the city, such as the airport, the central station, the major commercial streets, and the tourist attractions. You may compare their rates for various currencies online or on location.

Another method is using an ATM (or Bankomat or Uttagsautomat) to withdraw cash using your Visa, MasterCard, Maestro, or Cirrus card. Numerous ATMs are accessible around the city, notably at the airport, the central station, the major squares, and the retail centers. However, be aware that certain ATMs may charge a fee for your withdrawal or provide a dynamic currency conversion (DCC) service that offers you a poorer exchange rate than your card provider. Therefore, examining the fees and rates before you finalize your transaction is essential.

A third alternative is to use a service like Wise (previously TransferWise) to transfer money from your bank account to a local bank account in SEK at a cheap cost and a fair exchange rate. Wise is an internet platform that enables you to send and receive money across borders without hidden fees or markups. You may set up a free account online or via their app and gain access to their multi-currency account and debit card.

Banking in Gothenburg

Gothenburg has a sophisticated financial system extends to many other Scandinavian and Baltic parts of Europe. The 'big four' mentioned below are the biggest and most prevalent banks you'll likely find there:

- Nordea
- Handelsbanken
- SEB
- Swedbank

If you are heading to Gothenburg briefly, you may not need to create a bank account there. However, if you are expecting to stay longer or work there, consider establishing a bank account for convenience and security. To create a bank account in Gothenburg, you will need to have a valid passport or ID card, a personal identification number (personnummer), proof of residence (such as a rental contract or utility bill), and occasionally a proof of income (such as a payslip or tax return). You may also need to book an appointment with the bank branch of your choosing and fill out an application form.

Alternatively, you may utilize an online bank account like Wise to keep several currencies and make payments in SEK without fees or markups. You may also acquire a Wise debit card that lets you spend anywhere globally at a genuine currency rate.

Payment Methods in Gothenburg

Gothenburg is often considered one of the most cashless societies in the world. Most individuals prefer using cards or mobile payments over cash for their purchases. Several stores, cafés, and kiosks in Gothenburg only take cards or mobile payments and deny cash completely. Therefore, taking a card or a mobile device with you when you visit Gothenburg is important.

The most frequent cards accepted in Gothenburg are Visa and MasterCard. Some shops may also take American

Express or Diners Club cards, although they are less extensively accepted than Visa and MasterCard. To pay with your card in Gothenburg, you must have a chip and PIN card since the older magnetic stripe cards will not function. You can also utilize contactless payments for modest sums since most terminals in Gothenburg enable this functionality.

Swish and Apple Pay are the most frequent mobile payment applications used in Gothenburg. Swish is a Swedish software that enables you to transfer and receive money instantaneously using your phone number. You may connect your Swish account to your bank account and pay with your phone at numerous establishments in Gothenburg, such as restaurants, taxis, markets, and vending machines. Apple Pay is a worldwide software that enables you to pay with your iPhone or Apple Watch at any business that supports contactless payments. Connect your Apple Pay account to your credit or debit card and pay using your iPhone safely and effortlessly.

Communication and Internet connectivity in Gothenburg

Gothenburg is a city well-connected to the rest of the globe, with its contemporary and efficient communication and internet facilities. Whether you need to make a phone call, send an email, browse the web, or watch a TV program, you will find many alternatives and providers in Gothenburg. You need to know some things regarding communication and internet connectivity in Gothenburg.

Mobile phones

Mobile phones are extensively used in Sweden, and you may purchase a Swedish SIM card or a mobile phone package from one of the main carriers. You may choose pay-as-you-go (kontantkort) or contract (abonnement) programs based on your requirements and preferences. You will need a personal identification number (personnummer) to sign up for a contract plan.

Some of the main mobile phone companies in Gothenburg are:

• **Telia:** The biggest provider in Sweden, with vast coverage and a choice of plans and services. You may purchase a SIM card or a phone from one of their shops or online.

• **Tele2:** A service that provides low pricing and flexible options. You may purchase a SIM card or a phone from one of their shops or online.

• **Telenor:** A supplier that delivers high quality and customer service. You may purchase a SIM card or a phone from one of their shops or online.

• **3:** A provider that specializes in mobile internet and data. You may purchase a SIM card or a phone from one of their shops or online.

• **Comviq:** A supplier that provides low-cost and basic plans. You may purchase a SIM card from one of their shops or online.

Internet

Internet connection is generally accessible in Gothenburg, both via mobile and fixed networks. You may pick from numerous kinds of internet connections, such as broadband (broadband), fiber (fiber), cable (kabel), or wireless (trådlös). You may also discover free WiFi networks in many public venues, such as cafés, restaurants, hotels, libraries, and museums.

Some of the main internet providers in Gothenburg are:

• **Telia:** The biggest provider in Sweden, with vast coverage and a choice of plans and services. You may obtain broadband, fiber, cable, or wireless internet from them.

• **Bredbandsbolaget:** A provider that delivers fast and reliable internet over broadband, fiber, or cable. You may also obtain digital TV and landline phone services from them.

• **All Tele:** A provider that provides economical and flexible internet via broadband, fiber, or wireless. You may also obtain digital TV and landline phone services from them.

- **Tele2:** A provider with low pricing and flexible internet over broadband, fiber, or cable. You may also obtain digital TV and mobile phone services from them.

Digital TV

Digital TV is the main means of viewing TV in Sweden, and you may pick from many forms of digital TV services, such as terrestrial (markbunden), satellite (satellite), cable (kabel), or streaming (strömmande). You may also get several local and foreign channels via digital TV bundles or subscriptions.

Some of the biggest digital TV providers in Gothenburg are: obtain internet and mobile phone services from them.

- **Telia:** The biggest provider in Sweden, with broad coverage and a choice of digital TV options via cable or streaming. You may also obtain internet and mobile phone services from them.

- **Boxer:** A supplier that delivers digital TV services via terrestrial networks. You may also obtain broadband internet services from them.

- **Viasat:** A supplier that delivers digital TV services via satellite network. You may also obtain broadband internet services from them.

Customs and Etiquette in Gothenburg

Gothenburg is a city that has a distinct and dynamic culture influenced by its history, geography, and people. As a guest, you may meet certain conventions and manners different from what you are accustomed to, but also those familiar and simple to follow. Here are some of the traditions and manners of Gothenburg that can help you enjoy your stay and communicate with the people.

Greeting and communication

Gothenburgers are typically kind and courteous but also reserved and humble. They do not like to brag or show off and value honesty and sincerity. When welcoming someone, a strong handshake is the most typical type of greeting, followed by eye contact and a grin. You may alternatively say "hej" (hello) or "god dag" (good day). If you know the individual well, you may additionally embrace or kiss them on the cheek.

When interacting with Gothenburgers, you should speak clearly and quietly and avoid raising your voice or interrupting. Gothenburgers cherish personal space and privacy, so avoid standing too near or touching them needlessly. You should also avoid personal or sensitive themes, such as religion, politics, or money until you know the individual well. Gothenburgers are not extremely demonstrative with their emotions, so do not expect them to laugh aloud or weep readily. They may also utilize irony or sarcasm, so be cautious not to take anything literally.

Gothenburgers are proficient in English and Swedish, so you should be able to speak with them easily. However, it is always welcomed if you learn some simple Swedish words and phrases, such as "tack" (thank you), "ursäkta" (excuse me), or "skål" (cheers).

Dining and drinking

Gothenburg is a city that boasts a rich and diversified culinary scene, where you can discover restaurants and cafés that serve numerous cuisines and specialties. Some of the typical Swedish foods that you may enjoy in Gothenburg are:

Meatballs with mashed potatoes, lingonberry jam, and gravy

Herring with cooked potatoes and sour cream.

- Smörgåsbord is a buffet of cold and hot items, such as cheese, bread, ham, salmon, eggs, salads, pies, etc.
- Cinnamon buns, big pastries with cinnamon filling and sugar topping
- When eating in Gothenburg, you should respect certain fundamental politeness norms, such as:
- Arrive on time or somewhat early if you are invited to someone's house or a restaurant
- Wait for the host or hostess to ask you to sit down and start eating
- Use the cutlery from the outside inward
- Keep your hands visible on the table
- Do not chat with your mouth full or make sounds while eating
- Compliment the meal and the chef
- Offer to assist with cleaning the table or washing the dishes
- Do not leave any food on your plate
- Drinking is a typical social activity in Gothenburg, particularly on weekends. You may discover various taverns and pubs that serve a range of beers, wines, spirits, and cocktails. Some of the popular cocktails in Gothenburg are:

- Snaps, a powerful liquor that is generally flavored with herbs or spices
- Glögg, a mulled wine that is served hot with raisins and nuts
- Punsch, a sweet liqueur that is created from arrack
- Cider, a fermented apple juice that is typically blended with other fruits

When drinking in Gothenburg, you should obey certain fundamental politeness standards, such as:

- Wait for someone to propose a toast before drinking
- Look at the person who is toasting and say, "skål."
- Do not drink until everyone has their glasses lifted
- Do not drink too much or become intoxicated
- Do not drink and drive
- Shopping and tipping

Gothenburg is a city that provides a lot of shopping choices, where you can buy anything from high-end clothes to local handicrafts. Some of the top locations to shop in Gothenburg are:

1. Avenyn, the major avenue of Gothenburg, is where you can find some of the city's most popular and prominent stores, restaurants, pubs, and cafés.
2. Haga is one of the oldest and most picturesque areas in Gothenburg, where you can discover some of the greatest street art and unique businesses.//

3. Nordstan is one of the biggest shopping malls in Scandinavia, with over 200 stores, restaurants, cafés, and services under one roof.

4. Magasinsgatan is one of the trendiest avenues in Gothenburg, where you can discover some of the top fashion, design, and lifestyle stores and cafés.

When shopping in Gothenburg, you should obey certain fundamental politeness guidelines, such as:

- Check the businesses' opening hours since they may change based on the day and the season.
- Ask for permission before taking photographs or touching the product
- Bargaining is not frequent or expected, particularly at flea markets or street stalls

- Keep your receipts and invoices since you may need them for returns or refunds
- Pay with cash or credit card since checks are not generally accepted

Tipping is neither necessary nor anticipated in Gothenburg since service costs are frequently included in the bill. However, you may tip if you are happy with the service and want to thank you. Some of the typical tipping habits in Gothenburg are:

- Round up the cost to the closest 10 or 20 SEK in a cab or a bar
- Leave 5 to 10% of the bill at a restaurant or a café
- Leave 10 to 20 SEK each night in a hotel room
- Do not tip at quick food outlets or self-service venues

Conclusion

This is a description of the traditions and etiquette of Gothenburg that will help you enjoy your stay and communicate with the people. You should always respect the local culture and customs and be polite and respectful. You should also be open-minded, inquiring, and strive to learn from your experience. Gothenburg is a city that has a lot to offer, and by following certain conventions and etiquette, you will be able to make the most of it.

Useful Phrases and phrases in Sweden and Gothenburg

Gothenburg is a city that boasts a diversified and cosmopolitan population, where you may hear numerous languages and dialects. The official language of Sweden is Swedish, and most people speak it in Gothenburg. However, you may also encounter other languages, such as English, Finnish, Sami, Romani, and numerous immigrant languages. Here are some of the important words and terminology in Sweden, Gothenburg, and other languages used in Gothenburg that can help you communicate and understand the locals.

Swedish phrases and terms

Swedish is a Germanic language that is closely related to Danish and Norwegian. It includes 29 letters in its alphabet, including three additional vowels: å, ä, and ö. It also contains several peculiar sounds that may be difficult to say for English speakers, such as sj, tj, sk, and ng. Here are some of the fundamental Swedish words and terminology that you might use in Gothenburg:

- Hej (hey) - Hello
- God dag (good dahg) - Good day

- Hej då (hey doh) - Goodbye
- Tack (tack) - Thank you
- Snälla (snell-ah) - Please
- Ursäkta (oor-shake-tah) - Excuse me
- Förlåt (fur-loht) - Sorry
- Ja (yah) - Yes
- Nej (nay) - No
- Jag heter... (yahg heh-ter) - My name is...
- Vad heter du? (vahd heh-ter doo) - What is your name?
- Trevligt att träffas (treh-vleeht aht treh-fahs) - Nice to meet you
- Hur mår du? (hoor mor doo) - How are you?
- Jag mår bra (yahg mor brah) - I am fine
- Hur säger man... på svenska? (hoor say-er mahn... poh svehn-ska) - How do you say... in Swedish?
- Jag förstår inte (yahg fur-stor een-teh) - I don't understand
- Talar du engelska? (tah-lar doo ehn-gels-kah) - Do you speak English?
- Var är...? (vahr air...) - Where is...?

- Hur mycket kostar det? (hoor meek-et kohs-tar deh) - How much does it cost?
- Var är toaletten? (vahr air twah-leht-en) - Where is the toilet?
- Skål (skohl) – Cheers

Gothenburg phrases and terms

Gothenburg has its dialect of Swedish, which is affected by the city's history, geography, and inhabitants. It has various special qualities, such as:

- The use of gôtt or gôrgôtt instead of bra or mycket bra to mean good or very good
- The use of ja instead of jag means I
- The use of e instead of är to mean is or are
- The use of å instead of och means and
- The use of nej men hej instead of hej to mean hello when meeting someone unexpectedly

Here are some of the common Gothenburg phrases and terms that you can use or hear in Gothenburg:

- Gôtt mos! (goht Mohs) - Good food!
- Läget? (leh-get) - What's up?

- Göttans! (goht-tans) - Awesome!
- Göteborgare (yuh-teh-bor-gah-reh) - A person from Gothenburg
- Göteborgskan (yuh-teh-bor-skan) - The Gothenburg dialect
- Göteborgshumor (yuh-teh-bor-shoo-mor) - The Gothenburg humor
- Liseberg (lee-seh-behr-yeh) - The amusement park in Gothenburg
- Slottsskogen (sloht-sko-gen) - The park in Gothenburg
- Älvsborgsbron (ehlvs-bor-yeh-broon) - The bridge in Gothenburg

Other languages are spoken in Gothenburg.

Gothenburg is a city that boasts a diversified and cosmopolitan population, where you may hear numerous languages and dialects. Some of the other languages spoken in Gothenburg are:

English: English is commonly spoken and understood in Gothenburg and throughout the rest of Sweden. Many Swedes learn English from an early age and are proficient in it. You may also find numerous signs, menus, and information in English in Gothenburg.

Finnish is one of the official minority languages of Sweden, and it is spoken by certain persons in Gothenburg who have Finnish ancestry or background. There are also several Finnish schools, organizations, and media in Gothenburg.
Sami: Sami is another official minority language of Sweden, and it is spoken by certain persons in Gothenburg who belong to the Sami indigenous people of northern Scandinavia. There are also several Sami cultural events and groups in Gothenburg.

Romani: Romani is another official minority language of Sweden, and it is spoken by certain persons in Gothenburg who belong to the Romani ethnic group. There are also several Romani groups and media in Gothenburg.

Various immigrant languages: Gothenburg is a city that has a big immigrant population, and you may hear many different languages spoken by individuals who have arrived from various nations and areas. Some of the most prevalent immigrant languages in Gothenburg include

Arabic, Turkish, Kurdish, Persian, Somali, Bosnian, Serbian, Croatian, Polish, and Spanish.

Conclusion

This is a summary of the important words and concepts in Sweden, Gothenburg, and other languages used in Gothenburg that will help you communicate and understand the locals. You should always strive to acquire some fundamental words and phrases in Swedish and the Gothenburg dialect since this will demonstrate your respect and interest in the local culture and language. You should also be open-minded and interested in the various languages in Gothenburg since this will improve your experience and knowledge. Gothenburg is a city that has a wide and dynamic linguistic environment, and by following these words and terminology, you will be able to appreciate it completely.

CHAPTER 8: Resources and Links

The official website of Gothenburg tourism

Gothenburg is a city that has a lot to offer for tourists, from culture and history to nature and adventure. Whether searching for museums and theatres, parks and gardens, shopping and eating, or festivals and events, you will find something in Gothenburg. But how can you organize your vacation and maximize your time in Gothenburg? Where can you get the finest information and ideas about things to see and do in Gothenburg? The solution is simple: the official website of Gothenburg Tourism.

The official website of Gothenburg tourism is https://www.goteborg.com/en/, a comprehensive and user-friendly online resource that gives all you need to know about Gothenburg. You may visit the website from any device, such as a computer, a tablet, or a smartphone. You may also pick from various languages, such as English, Swedish, German, French, Spanish, Italian, Chinese, Japanese, and more.

The official website of Gothenburg Tourism is organized into different areas, such as:

Discover a part that exposes you to Gothenburg's numerous elements and attractions, such as the districts and neighborhoods, the culture and art, the environment and outdoors, the shopping and entertainment, and more. You may also discover inspiration and recommendations for your vacation, such as the top 10 lists, seasonal highlights, themed guides, and more.

Plan: a feature that helps you plan your vacation and book your hotel and transportation in Gothenburg. You may also discover some practical information and recommendations on how to move about Gothenburg, how to use public transit, how to hire a bike or a vehicle, how to locate parking places, how to use Wi-Fi, how to use the currency and payment methods, how to deal with emergencies, and more.

Experience: a part that shows you things to see and do in Gothenburg, depending on your interests and choices. You may browse several categories, such as museums and galleries, parks and gardens, restaurants and cafes, bars and clubs, concerts and performances, sports and activities, markets and fairs, festivals and events, and more. You may also narrow your search by date, location, price, or rating.

Bargains is a section that offers excellent bargains and discounts on your accommodation and transportation in Gothenburg. You may also discover some special deals on attractions and activities in Gothenburg. You may also acquire the Gothenburg Pass, a card that provides you free entrance to over 30 sites in Gothenburg;

Bargains: a section that offers amazing bargains and discounts on your accommodation and transportation in Gothenburg. You may also discover some special deals on attractions and activities in Gothenburg. You can also buy the Gothenburg Pass, a card that gives you free admission to over 30 attractions in Gothenburg, such as the Liseberg Amusement Park, the Universeum Science Center, the Museum of World Culture, the Gothenburg Art Museum, the Gothenburg City Museum, the Gothenburg Maritime Museum, the Volvo Museum, the Botanical Garden, the Slottsskogen Zoo, and more.

You can also enjoy free public transit, hop-on hop-off bus and boat trips, free guided walking tours, and discounts on restaurants and stores. You may pick from numerous lengths, such as 24 hours, 48 hours, 72 hours, or 120 hours.

The price for adults runs from 395 SEK to 995 SEK and for children from 245 SEK to 595 SEK.

Contact: a part that offers important contact information and resources for your journey to Gothenburg. You can discover the location, phone number, email, and opening hours of the tourist information centers in Gothenburg. You may also find connections to the social media profiles of Gothenburg Tourism, such as Facebook, Instagram, Twitter, YouTube, and Pinterest. You may also subscribe to the email of Gothenburg Tourist or download the app of Gothenburg Tourism.

The official website of Gothenburg tourism is https://www.goteborg.com/en/, a comprehensive and user-friendly online resource that gives all you need to know about Gothenburg. You may visit the website from any device, such as a computer, a tablet, or a smartphone. You may also pick from various languages, such as English, Swedish, German, French, Spanish, Italian, Chinese, Japanese, and more. Whether you are seeking inspiration and recommendations, practical information and advice, or bargains and discounts for your vacation to Gothenburg, you will find it on the official website of Gothenburg Tourism.

Maps and Apps for Gothenburg Navigation

Gothenburg is a simple city to explore, owing to its well-organized public transit system, bike-friendly infrastructure, and pedestrian-friendly streets. However, if you want to make the most of your time and explore the city at your leisure, you may want to utilize certain maps and applications to help you navigate your way about Gothenburg. Here are some of the maps and applications for Gothenburg navigation:

Offline Maps

To avoid costly roaming costs or unpredictable Wi-Fi connections, you may wish to download an offline map of Gothenburg before you leave or utilize your hotel's Wi-Fi. An offline map lets you view a comprehensive and interactive city map without requiring data or internet connection. You may also utilize GPS position, route planning, search, and bookmarking capabilities on an offline map.

One of the offline maps that you may use for Gothenburg is Gothenburg Map and Walks1, an app that shows you many self-guided city tours presenting the finest of the city. It comes with precise walk route maps and strong navigation tools. You may also acquire a fully working downloadable city map that includes all the sights mentioned in the tours. Another offline map that you may use for Gothenburg is the Gothenburg offline map, an app that gives a high-resolution map of the city that contains all the major roads and most urban roads. You may also utilize functions like search, bookmark, route, and zooming on this app.

Online Maps

If you have a stable data or internet connection, you may utilize an online map of Gothenburg that gives you real-time information and updates. An online map enables you to obtain a complete and up-to-date city map containing all the attractions, services, and facilities you may require. You may also utilize traffic, transportation, satellite, street view, and reviews on an online map.

One of the online maps that you may use for Gothenburg is Google Maps, a web-based tool that gives a thorough and dynamic map of the city. You may also utilize services such as directions, navigation, location sharing, and offline maps on this service. Another online map you may use for Gothenburg is Bing Maps, a web-based tool that gives a rich and interactive city map. On this service, you may also utilize features such as 3D view, aerial view, bird's eye view, and street side view.

Transport Apps

If you wish to utilize public transport in Gothenburg, you can use several travel applications to help you plan your journeys and pay for your tickets. Transport applications enable you to access information such as schedules, routes, rates, and interruptions for buses, trams, ferries, and trains in Gothenburg. You may also utilize tools such as travel planners, live departures, maps, and notifications on transit applications.

One of the transport applications that you may use for Gothenburg is Västtrafik To Go, an app that enables you to purchase single tickets or period tickets for public transport in Gothenburg. You may also utilize tools such as trip planner, favorite routes, and travel history on this app.

Another transport tool you may use for Gothenburg is Res I STHLM, an app that lets you plan your excursions and compare various forms of transport in Gothenburg. You may also utilize features like real-time information, traffic status, and neighboring stops on this app.

CONCLUSION

This is the conclusion of the Gothenburg travel guide, and we hope that you have liked reading it and found it helpful and instructive. We have addressed some of the most crucial features of visiting Gottenburg, such as:

- The history and culture of Gothenburg and how it has shaped its identity and character

- The best time and ways to travel to Gothenburg and how to get around the city and its surroundings

- The top attractions and activities in Gottenburg, and how to make the most of your time and budget

- The best places to stay, eat, drink, and shop in Gottenburg, and how to experience the local lifestyle and cuisine.

- The visa requirements, customs, and etiquette in Gottenburg, and how to respect the local culture and traditions.

We have also supplied you with some helpful links and sites where you may obtain additional information and assistance in arranging your vacation to Gothenburg. We have also offered suggestions and guidance on how to enjoy your stay and engage with the locals.

Gothenburg is a city that has a lot to offer, whether you are seeking culture, nature, nightlife, or adventure. It is a city that will surprise you and make you love it. It is a city that greets you with open arms and a warm welcome.

Our guide has motivated you to plan your vacation to Gottenburg and experience its sights and activities. Our information has helped you plan your vacation to Gottenburg and make it memorable. We hope our guide has been your companion throughout your trip to Gothenburg and made it pleasant and hassle-free.

Thank you for reading this information, and we hope to see you soon in Gothenburg.

Printed in Great Britain
by Amazon